Anonymous

Souvenir of the novitate

Anonymous

Souvenir of the novitate

ISBN/EAN: 9783337775414

Printed in Europe, USA, Canada, Australia, Japan

Cover: Foto ©ninafisch / pixelio.de

More available books at **www.hansebooks.com**

SOUVENIR

OF

THE NOVITIATE.

"Do not therefore lose your confidence, which hath a great reward."—*Heb. x*, 35.

Translated from the French by

REV. EDWARD I. TAYLOR.

APPROVED BY

HIS EMINENCE, THE CARDINAL ARCHBISHOP
OF NEW YORK.

NEW YORK, CINCINNATI, AND ST. LOUIS:
BENZIGER BROTHERS,
Printers to the Holy Apostolic See.

1880.

Imprimatur.

✠ JOHN, CARDINAL MCCLOSKEY,
    Archbishop of New York.

Stereotyped and Printed at the
BOYS' PROTECTORY,
West Chester, N. Y.

Copyright, 1879, by BENZIGER BROTHERS.

Approbation of the Bishop of Versailles.

The "Souvenir of the Novitiate" appears to us to be an excellent guide for young Religious, who are devoted to teaching. The most practical points of religious life are treated in it, in a precise and solid way. We can not too much recommend the reading of this little book to the members of teaching congregations, for whom it is especially intended.

✠ PETER,
Bishop of Versailles.
VERSAILLES, June 26th, 1875.

Approbation of the Bishop of Wilmington, Delaware.

The book called "Souvenir du Noviciat," approved by the Rt. Rev. Bishop of Versailles, in France, and translated into English by a priest of our diocese, is intended as a guide for those Religious who are engaged in the instruction of youth, and it deserves high commendation for its practical use. We approve of its publication, and heartily renew the approbation already given.

✠ THOMAS A. BECKER,
Bishop of Wilmington.
Feast of St. Stanislaus Kostka, 1878.

CONTENTS.

	PAGE.
THE NOVITIATE.	9
What a Novice, who Enters the Community, ought to be	11
Importance of the Time which Follows the Novitiate	13
Only Novices of Good-Will Advance in Perfection	15
Lesson to be Learned from the Phrase, "I am no longer in the Novitiate"	17
Contrast between two Novices, one of whom Perseveres in the Resolutions made in the Novitiate, and the other Abandons them	18
How many are Interested in the Perseverance of a Religious in the Dispositions which Animated him on leaving the Novitiate	21
It is not all at once that One Loses the Good Dispositions of the Novitiate	22
Signs of Relaxation in Young Religious	24
To a Young Religious who is Growing Tepid	27
What must be Done when you find yourself falling into Relaxation	29
PERSEVERANCE.	31
Means of Perseverance.—Preserve Always a lively Horror of Sin	33
Correspond Faithfully with Grace	35
Desire to Advance in Perfection	39
Faithful Observance of the Rule	42

CONTENTS.

	PAGE.
Flee from the World: be Prudent in your Necessary Intercourse with Externs	45
Preserve and Increase the Interior Spirit	48
Perform all your Actions with Great Purity of Intention	51
Make your Spiritual Exercises with Great Care	54
Make your Meditation well	57
Make the Particular Examen, and that of the Evening, with Great Care	59
Go to Confession Regularly, and with Holy Dispositions	65
Fervently Approach Holy Communion	67
Have Great Openness of Conscience	70
Practise Modesty, Recollection, and Silence	72
Preserve the Spirit of Piety	75
Generously Practise Mortification	77
Keep in the Sentiments of Humility which you have Gained in the Novitiate	81
Carefully Practise Religious Poverty	83
Regulate your Conduct by Obedience, and Give yourself up to the Will of your Superiors without Reserve	85
Excel in the Practice of Chastity	88
Means of Preserving Chastity	89
Strive to Acquire Fraternal Charity	93
Truly Love the Community	96
Have Great Zeal for the Salvation of Souls	98
Love Admonitions, and Profit by them	100
Do not be too much Afraid of Temptations	102
Know how to Profit by your Faults	105
What must be done so as not to be discouraged at our faults	107
Continue, through Life, the Struggle against your Faults which should have been Commenced in the Novitiate	109

PAGE.

Struggle, especially, against your Ruling Fault, and Strive to Acquire the Opposite Virtue - - - - - 111
Do not Follow Bad Example - - - 113
Application to Work.—Love of Study - 115

MONTHLY RETREAT. - - - - 119
Way to Make the Monthly Retreat - - 120
Preparatory Meditation for the Monthly Retreat - - - - - - 125
Material for Examination in the Monthly Retreat - - - - - - - 128
Act of Renovation - - - - - 138
Preparation for Death - - - - 140
Act of Resignation to Death - - - 144
Prayer to Beg the Grace of a Happy Death 145

OF OUR EMPLOYMENT. - - - 147
Dispositions in which we Ought to be, in Regard to Different Employments - - 147
The Esteem and Love which we Should Have for Obscure Employments - 149
To Desire a High Office, even with the Idea of doing Good in it, is often an Illusion - - - - - - 150
Of the Manner of Discharging our Duties 152
What a Religious, Employed in Manual Labor, Ought to do, to Render his Work Sweet and Meritorious - - - 155
Jesus at Nazareth the Consolation of a Religious Charged with a Temporal Employment - - - - - - 156

ON THE DUTY OF TEACHING. - - 160
Sublimity of the Duties of a Religious Teacher of Youth - - - - 160

	PAGE.
What a Christian School Ought to be	163
What a Christian Teacher should Propose to Himself	166
Reward of Religious Devoted to Teaching	169
The Love which a Young Teacher Should Have for his Duties, and the Zeal with which he should Discharge them	172
How useful Piety is to a Teacher	175
Obligation of a Teacher to Give Good Example to his Pupils	177
Obligation of a Teacher to Apply to Study	179
Dangers against which a Young Teacher Should Arm Himself	183
General Means Suitable for Securing the Success of a Religious whose Life is devoted to Teaching	180
Principal Means of Keeping Order in Class	187
Important Advice	189
Conduct, when you do not Succeed in Class	190
Consoling Thoughts, which a Teacher, who does not Succeed in his Office, should Meditate upon	192

OF CATECHISM. — 197

Excellence of the Catechism	197
What it is to Give Catechism	201
Under what Conditions we can Give Catechism well	203
The Study of Catechism	207
Important Advice to the Young Catechist	210
Advice on the Way to Give Catechism and to Make the Reflections in a Little Class	218
Profit by the Occasions which Present themselves, to Inculcate the Maxims of Christianity	220

	PAGE.
INFIDELITY TO THE RELIGIOUS VOCATION.	222
Weakening of the Esteem of One's Vocation.—Its Causes and Consequences	222
Ingratitude and Danger of a Religious who is Unfaithful to his Vocation	227
Conduct in Temptations against our Vocation	229
Advice of St. Francis of Sales on our Conduct relating to Disgust for our Vocation	232
OF THE VOWS.	235
Excellence of the Vows	235
The Vows Render the Works of a Religious far more Meritorious	238
The Vows are a Valuable Help against Inconstancy	242
To a Religious who has had the Happiness of Making his Vows	244
Of the Annual Renovation of Vows	246
How Profitable it is to Renew our Vows	250
To a Young Religious who is Preparing for the First Vows	252
Of the Merit of our Good Works, and of the Application which we can Make of them	257
Of Practices of Devotion	263
Of the Way in which a Religious should Practise Special Devotions	266
Of Indulgences	267
Of Ejaculatory Prayers	270
The Apostleship of Prayer	271
Union with the Perpetual Sacrifice of Jesus Christ	274
Practical Advice on the Way of Making our Evening Prayer	275

THE NOVITIATE.

The novitiate is generally well made; there a person is pious, exact in the exercises, faithful in little things; the sacraments are approached with fervor. Obedience costs the novice very little; manifestation of conscience is a necessity; he is indifferent to everything; zealous for his spiritual advancement, and ardently desirous to labor for the sanctification of souls; in a word, the novice gives the best hopes for the future, and one might almost say what was said of the holy Precursor of our Lord: "What an one, think ye, shall this child be?" In fact, it is certain that, if he always walked in the same track, if he labored with the same zeal to build up the spiritual edifice, of which he has laid the foundations so well, he would certainly arrive at a very high degree of virtue, and even of perfection.

And why should he not do this? Is it because it is not always a question of the glory of God, of his own salvation, and eternity?

"But," says Fr. de la Colombière, "in proportion as we advance in age, we decrease in virtue, and, particularly, in simplicity and fervor. In proportion as the number of the benefits of God is increased, our love and our gratitude grow cold. Why give up the virtues of the novice? I acknowledge that they are not enough—we must add others to them; but far from disdaining the first, we must, on the contrary, labor constantly to strengthen them in us."

"Unfortunately," says the Ven. J. B. de la Salle, "there are light and unstable souls who seem to have begun well, but have not the courage to persevere in their first feelings. During the novitiate they seemed to find nothing difficult, either in the practice of the rules, or in the conditions of obedience: they persevere in these dispositions, even during the first years; but then they grow lax, lose by little and little the spirit of faith, and of the presence of God; they delight no longer in prayer or meditation; they scarcely practise modesty and recollection any more; their heart dries up, and soon loses all taste for perfection, and, above all, for obedience. Then, given up to themselves, these souls become weak and powerless, and know not how to bear any longer the yoke of the Lord! Ah! how pitiable, when, having put our hand to the plough, we look back, and give up the holy practices of obedience !

"May we not apply to you the words of St. Paul: 'Are ye so foolish that, whereas ye began in the Spirit, ye would now be made perfect by the flesh'? (Gal. iii, 3.)

"Let it not be so with you; on the contrary, persevere in generosity and fervor. 'Do not therefore lose your confidence,' gained during the novitiate, 'which hath a great reward.'" (Heb. x, 35.)

Act so, we say with the Ven. J. B. de la Salle, "that your principal virtues are firmness and fidelity in the practice of good. Take care not to relax in anything; always beg for that firmness and fidelity which are so necessary to obtain the gift of perseverance."

What a Novice, who Enters the Community, ought to be.

1 During the novitiate, the young religious ought to have laid the solid foundations of the spiritual edifice.

2. He ought to have a great esteem for his state of life, to apply himself carefully to observe the rules which are peculiar to his position.

3. He ought to have great deference for his brethren, and a religious respect for superiors; he should often consult the latter, and set himself to follow their advice.

4. He should do all in his power to make himself useful, and acquit himself with great care of the duties intrusted to him.

5. He should be obedient, modest, silent, pious, and always preserve the ardent desire of doing well.

6. He should make all his exercises with an irreproachable exactness and religious application; his demeanor in chapel, in the community, and in class, should spread everywhere around him the good odor of Jesus Christ.

7. Full of charity, he should use his eyes only to see the good of which he is a witness; he should shut them to everything which might not seem conformable to duty; and, if he speaks of it, it should only be to his superiors.

He ought, above all, to persuade himself that his virtue is but slightly solid; that the least dangers and the smallest trials may be dangerous to him; and that he can preserve himself in virtue, only by continued watchfulness, and by the greatest fidelity to the prescriptions of our holy rules.

THE NOVITIATE. 13

Happy is the novice who goes into community life with such dispositions! Examine your heart, and see with what sentiments it is animated.

Importance of the Time which Follows the Novitiate.

"The year which immediately follows the novitiate," said Fr. Lallemant to his novices, "is very dangerous, especially the first three or four months: it is a critical time, on which the whole life depends."

St. Ignatius says: "He who passes from a very warm place to another which is cold or damp, is easily attacked, if he does not take care, by the impression of the air. In the same manner, he who passes from the novitiate into community life, is exposed to lose his fervor in a short time; for, the impressions of grace not being yet strengthened by habit, it is impossible, if one does not take great precautions, that they should not soon grow weaker, and then disappear altogether."

St. Vincent de Paul feared nothing so much as to see the novices of his congregation lose their fervor on leaving the novitiate. He said that the passing from spiritual exercises to the active life is always dangerous for those who do not practise great vigilance over themselves.

He who is preoccupied too much with his new employment, who neglects prayer, the presence of God, manifestation of conscience, and who allows himself voluntary faults, impulses of vanity, and slight sensualities, will soon find disgust and dryness, and will be exposed to dangerous temptations. Note well that, generally speaking, a young religious is so much the more inclined to get rid of every troublesome practice, in proportion as he has been more regular and exact during the first year of probation. He seems to think that everything ought to be permitted to him, because he is no longer in the novitiate: as if there were not a strict obligation to redouble his piety, modesty, recollection, and watchfulness over himself, in proportion as the dangers are multiplied under his steps!

Great attention, then, to yourself; perfect fidelity to all your duties! It is to novices who have recently been placed in the community that these words are most admirably suitable: "I say unto you, Watch."

Only Novices of Good-Will Advance in Perfection.

However pious and fervent you have been during the novitiate, you ought always to fear that you may not persevere in such happy dispositions, and work out, as the apostle says, your salvation with fear and trembling.

Experience teaches that, in the ways of virtue, without an exceptional generosity, we relax rather than improve with time. The moral man, good and even excellent in principle, goes back much more to evil than he advances in good. For one saint, who ascends generously every day from virtue to virtue, there is a multitude of cowards who go back, and to whom may be applied this passage from the "Imitation of Christ:" "If, every year, we root out one vice, we should soon be perfect. But we often feel, on the contrary, that we were better, and our lives more pure, when we left the world, than after many years of profession. We ought every day to increase in virtue and fervor; and now, we consider it a great thing to have preserved a part of our first fervor."

"The beginnings," says the eloquent Bishop of Clermont, "are usually fervent and faithful; one lays the first foundations of the edifice with a zeal and vivacity which seem not able to belie themselves; we reproach ourselves for those relaxations which are most allowed: we have a horror of the slightest infidelities; we walk with giant strides in the way of the Lord; nothing costs us anything; nothing stops us; we devour, as it were, the bitterness of obedience; we feel no longer the subjection to the rules; we fly everywhere, whither obedience or duty calls us; we add even, to our prescribed duties, works of supererogation; in fine, nothing seems too much to the zeal and fervor which are beginning.

"But, after these first years passed in fervor, we think we have a right to rest; we leave that too rigorous exactness for those who are beginning; we look upon relaxations and infidelities as the privilege of time and years; we come down to a kind of life more suitable to the senses and love of self; we quietly allow ourselves omissions, of which we were very scrupulous before; in fine, we persuade ourselves that the time of fervor is passed, and that it is only for beginners to observe the rules and holy practices in all their perfection and extent."

With fervor and regularity happiness disappears; peace of soul flies away, and anguish of mind, with its sharp stings, takes its place! May heaven grant that you may never prove in yourself the truth of this prediction!

Lesson to be Learned from the Phrase, "I am no longer in the Novitiate."

I am no longer in the novitiate! This means that, far from my obligations becoming less, I have contracted new and more important ones.

I am no longer in the novitiate! That is to say that, after having employed a whole year in forming myself in religious virtues, it is no longer allowed to me to plead the want of knowledge.

I am no longer in the novitiate! Then it is not enough for me not to forget what I have learned in the novitiate; for, if it would be a shame for a scholar not to find himself more advanced at the end of his course than he was at the commencement, it would be far more shameful still for me to pass months and years without making any progress in the science of the saints. But it would be infinitely deplorable, infinitely miserable, for me, if, every day, I go backward in the way of virtue; if, after so many confessions, communions, counsels, and so many graces, I were to go back instead of going forward!

I am no longer in the novitiate! Therefore, I ought to be more fervent and more faithful than when I was there: then I was an apprentice, now I ought to be a mechanic.

Weigh well all these consequences, so contrary to those which the devil may suggest to you, by leading you to imagine that you are no longer bound to so exact a modesty, to so perfect a regularity, to so diligent a care of your spiritual exercises, or to so pronounced an aversion to little faults.

Contrast between two Novices, one of whom Perseveres in the Resolutions made in the Novitiate, and the other Abandons them.

Two young religious, equally called by God, who have advanced, during their novitiate, with equal steps in the way of perfection, are sent on the mission: one walks with fidelity in the way which has been traced out for him; the other wanders away. What will become of them at the end of a few years?

The first, distrustful of self, putting his

trust in God, goes forward carefully; if he commit any fault, he accuses himself of it, and rises quickly; he advances at all times in the right way; he encourages in his soul an ever-increasing desire of laboring for the sanctification of his own soul, and of that of his neighbor.

Generously fulfilling the duties of his state of life, he has its consolation and merit; his conscience, like that of the just man, is a continual feast; if he meets with some trials, however hard, he lays them at the foot of the cross, where they lose their bitterness. Cherished by his pupils, esteemed by his brothers in religion, honored with the confidence of his superiors, blessed by God, he goes everywhere doing good, and prepares an abundant harvest for a glorious eternity.

What happens, on the other hand, to him who, after having zealously labored during the commencement of religious life, allows negligence by degrees to take the place of fervor? He becomes frivolous, vain, oversensitive, not being able to bear anything which humbles him, or goes against his inclination. His exercises suffer; his communions, less fervent, bring him less sweetness and fewer graces; he gives up, one by one, his pious practices. Far from making known his faults, he conceals them, and soon becomes a hypocrite. He presents to his brethren and superiors the sad spectacle of a terrible relaxation.

Finding no longer his consolation in God, he seeks it in creatures; he enjoys only the satisfaction of the senses and of self-love. He regards no longer his vocation, employment, or his trials, with the eye of faith. His conscience loses its delicacy; his slight faults prepare the way for more serious ones. In a word, by a tepid, cowardly, and irregular life, he scandalizes his brethren; destroys, one by one, the hopes which he had inspired, and puts it out of his power to do any good to his pupils, makes for himself all kinds of anxieties and troubles, and exposes his vocation and salvation to danger!

What a difference, in one year, in ten years, between these two young people, who had left the novitiate with like dispositions! What a difference during life! What a difference, especially after death!

What will you do? What would you wish to have done at the end of your career? Think seriously of this, and direct your first steps to that end; for it is on the end that your whole life depends.

How many are Interested in the Perseverance of a Religious in the Dispositions which Animated him on leaving the Novitiate!

1. Our Lord, who gave his blood and his life to purchase for us the perfection for which God has destined us, and who does not wish to lose the fruit of his death.

2. The most holy Virgin, who obtains for us so many graces to make us perfect, and who expects that one day we shall be her glory and her crown.

3. Our good angels, who employ themselves with so much zeal in order to guide us in the ways of holiness, in order that they may have us for companions in a blessed eternity.

4. Our holy patrons, our venerable founder, our brethren, and the other friends whom we have in heaven, who desire, with so much ardor, that we should walk in their footsteps, and who help us so powerfully with their intercession.

5. The souls in purgatory, who would receive much more assistance from us, if we were more perfect.

6. The Church, to which we should be

much more useful, if we had arrived at the degree of sanctity to which we are called.

7. The community, which we would serve better, if we had more union with God.

8. Our pupils, whom we only help to sanctify, in proportion as we are saints.

9. Our families, and society in general, to which we shall only be useful, inasmuch as we are good religious.

How many souls God will show us, that he has saved by our means, if we have been perfect instruments in promoting his glory! How many will he make us see whom we might have helped to sanctify, if we ourselves had been saints! How many others, who have remained long in purgatory, and who would have been delivered much sooner, if our works had been of greater merit before him!

Oh! what good is not a novice called to do who understands the sublimity of his mission, and the powerful motives which urge him to fulfil it!

It is not all at once that one Loses the Good Dispositions of the Novitiate.

Here, according to the author of the "Soul raised to God," is the way which every religious, who loses his fervor, generally follows. He relaxes little by little, becomes careless, and disgusted with piety; and ends by throwing away grace, and struggling with remorse.

To-day, he gives up one practice; to-morrow, he omits another; to-day, he falls into an infidelity; to-morrow, a greater infidelity follows. Henceforward, there is less vigilance, less recollection, more cowardliness, more dissipation, more repugnance for good, and more inclination to evil. How much advance has already been made in the way of relaxation ! Nevertheless, the burden seems heavier day by day, the yoke becomes more severe, he can bear it no longer; he drags it along in a languishing way; perhaps he complains loudly of its weight ! He shakes it off, as much as he can; and, by a change as sad as it is deplorable, he frequently becomes so much the more relaxed, as he had been more exact and virtuous.

How many young religious are there whose portrait is traced in these few words ! Formerly, they were reserved, and feared even the shadow of evil; now, they run, like blind men, in the way of perdition ! . . . Let them examine the way which they have gone, and the point from which they started; let them go back to the source of the evil, and they will find a shortened prayer, a neglected practice, a pious exercise left off: this is the beginning. Impulses of grace abused, remorse of conscience stifled: this is the progress. A more decided infidelity, a more serious fault; a fall followed, perhaps, by many others: this is the fatal end! What will be the issue?

Meditate, besides, the serious and prudent words of Father Lallemant, in his "Spiritual Doctrine:" "The ruin of souls comes from the multiplicity of venial sins, which cause the diminution of lights and divine inspirations, of graces and interior consolations, and of fervor and courage in resisting the attacks of the enemy. Thence follow spiritual blindness, weakness, frequent falls, habit, and insensibility, because, the habit once acquired, one sins without feeling the sin."

If, then, you wish to persevere, fear slight faults, and be faithful to little things.

Signs of Relaxation in Young Religious.

1. To neglect the resolutions made in the novitiate, and to lose, by degrees, the use of the pious practices which we had adopted there.

2. To neglect prayer in a notable manner;

not to make the remote or proximate preparation for it; not to follow the method prescribed; not to propose any special end; not to make any resolutions, or to make them in a vague way, and not to think of them during the day; to make our meditation, only that we may say that it has been made.

3. To hide our faults; to dissemble our failures; to have difficulty in acknowledging our mistakes; to take ill the warnings of superiors; to give scarcely any manifestation of conscience, for want of sincerity, or of fidelity to the advice which we have received.

4. To neglect to prepare for the reception of the sacraments; to be little troubled at not drawing profit from them; to confess and go to communion, as if we were performing a common action; perhaps, even in the fear of being noticed, or only to do as others do.

5. To recite our prayers without attention and fervor; to behave in chapel, and during spiritual exercises, with coldness and levity, giving no external mark of piety.

6. Not to have for superiors, and particularly for our director, the submission and confidence prescribed by the holy rules. Instead of looking upon them as the representatives of God, only to see in them men more or

less learned, more or less virtuous; to study maliciously their way of acting; to criticize their acts by thinking or speaking ill of them, and to listen willingly to those who find fault with their conduct.

7. Not to make the particular examen. except for form's sake; not to use it to combat our predominant fault; and to let this powerful means of sanctification become utterly useless.

8. Not to be troubled about venial faults, and to commit them coolly, and without scruples of conscience.

9. To keep scarcely any account of interior graces, lights, inspirations, good impulses, attraction to good, or salutary remorse; to deprive ourselves of these graces by the abuse of them, and to find ourselves reduced to a state of dryness, coldness, and insensibility toward God,—a state which can be changed only with great difficulty.

10. To be full of faults, and to do nothing to correct them; to take ill the advice of charitable persons who notice them; to argue with these persons, to prove that they are deceived, and thus to encourage in ourselves a spiritual hardness, which is morally without remedy.

11. Not to apply ourselves to the duties of

our employment; to lose time, to neglect the religious instruction of our pupils, and the watchfulness which should be kept over them; or, again, to labor with ardor, but with human aims.

12. To love to appear in the world; to fail greatly in the custody of the eyes; to seek to please; and, in order to do this, to give a studied, affected, and worldly air to our toilet, manner, and walk.

It is not necessary, in order to constitute this deplorable state of tepidity, that all these signs of relaxation should be found together: some of them, which you may perceive in yourself, should be enough to cause you great fear.

To a Young Religious who is Growing Tepid.

After having courageously borne the yoke of the Lord, could you fall away from your first fervor?

Would you wish to end with the flesh, when you have begun with the spirit?

Is God less worthy to be loved, respected, honored, and obeyed, now than when you consecrated yourself to his service?

Have you been more content since you have been less generous?

Whither will the broad way of relaxation, which you are entering, lead you?

Tepidity has overthrown those who were higher and stronger than cedars: frail sapling, how can you resist, and stand?

From negligence to negligence, from fault to fault, you will fall into the abyss of sin.

You will soon be disgusted with a vocation, of which you no longer fulfil the duties.

You will be lost, like so many others.

Tremble at the sight of the dangers which threaten you.

Apply to yourself those terrible words which St. John, by order of God, addressed to the Bishop of Ephesus: "I have somewhat against thee, because thou hast left thy first charity. Be mindful, therefore, from whence thou art fallen, and do penance, and do the first works; or else I come to thee, and will move thy candlestick out of its place, except thou do penance." (Apoc. ii, 4, 5.)

Retrace your steps; you can still do so; soon it will be too late. Think of this!

Read the "Imitation of Christ," Book I, ch. xxv.

THE NOVITIATE. 29

What must be Done when you Find yourself falling into Relaxation.

1. Enter seriously into yourself.
2. Try to understand the depth of the abyss into which you are falling.
3. Meditate seriously on the preceding considerations, on the importance of persevering in the dispositions which you had in the novitiate.
4. Make a general confession, at least going back as far as the beginning of your tepidity.
5. Make clearly known to your director the state of your soul, and faithfully put in practice the counsels which he may give, even when it seems very hard to follow them: to great evils great remedies must be applied. When one has a true desire of doing better, he does not count the pain.
6. Undertake some special pious practices toward the Blessed Virgin and St. Joseph, to obtain the grace of recovering your first fervor.
7. If necessary, lay before your superiors your desire of spending some time in the novitiate, in order to renew your piety. How many are there who owe to a few days of retreat their perseverance and salvation!

8. Keep constantly on your guard, in order to avoid the faults and negligences which have been the cause of relaxation!

9. Urge yourself strongly forward; say from the bottom of your heart: "Behold I make all things new." (Apoc. xxi, 5.) Cry out with the prophet: "Perfect thou my goings in thy paths: that my footsteps be not moved." (Ps. xvi, 5.) "Command thy strength, O God: confirm, O God, what thou hast wrought in us." (Ps. lxvii, 29.)

PERSEVERANCE.

The important thing is, not to begin well, but to end well. (St. Augustine.) In the building of an edifice, the most difficult thing is, not to lay the foundation, but successfully to place the last stone.

It will not serve you to have begun well, if you end badly.

St. Paul began ill, but finished well.

Judas, having begun in a praiseworthy way, ended by his reprobation.

The crown is promised, not to him who has made a good beginning, but to him who has lived holily to the last day of his life.

At an age which was still tender, you had the courage to make the most generous sacrifices and bear the hardest trials ; and, after two, three, five, or ten years, you grow feeble, you retrace your steps. What ingratitude ! what cowardice ! what folly !

" It is now fourscore years and ten that I have served Jesus Christ," said a holy bishop and martyr, "and he has always treated me well ; and now, shall I renounce him, shall I leave his service ? No, no ; a hundred times, no ! "

Use always the same words, "courage and perseverance."

If you have the misfortune to turn back on your steps, after having begun well, you will have to appear one day before Him who said: "He that shall deny me before men, I will also deny him before my Father, who is in heaven." (Matt. x, 33.)

To justify your infidelity, you would say to him: "It costs me too much to obey; men had too little consideration for me; it was necessary to bear too many injustices, humiliations, and privations; my employment was too hard; I was exposed to calumny, persecution!"

What excuses to present to a God deprived of all, scourged, crowned with thorns, nailed to the cross!

"It behooved Christ to suffer, that he might enter into his glory," and you would suffer nothing! The servant is not above his master!

Do the holy religious who are in heaven repent that they sacrificed liberty, pleasures, and honors?

What do those who are in hell think, who are lost because they sought enjoyments, so deceitful and transient, here below?

What would you wish to have done at your death?

"If you do not wish to fail in the trial, remember the reward which follows. The gardener would often lose courage at his work, if he did not recall to mind the wages which he is to receive for his labor. Do you, too, remember the reward which God has prepared for you, and you will look upon all you have to suffer as a mere trifle." (St. Augustine.)

"Look up to heaven: do not change it for the earth. Look up to Jesus Christ: do not renounce him for the world. Look up at eternity: do not lose it for a single moment." (De Ravignan.)

"So run that you may obtain." (1 Cor. x, 24.)

"For he also, that striveth for the mastery, is not crowned, except he strive lawfully." (2 Tim. ii, 5.)

"Be thou faithful unto death, and I will give thee the crown of life." (Apoc. ii, 10.)

Means of Perseverance.—Preserve Always a Lively Horror of Sin.

One of the most salutary and lasting fruits which you ought to derive from the instructions which you heard in the novitiate, and of the precious graces which were there lavished upon you, is a lively horror of sin, and a generous resolution to die a thousand times rather than commit it.

In embracing the religious life, you received a second robe of innocence : never soil it, faithfully guard this inestimable treasure. Woe to you if you lose, by little and little, the delicacy of conscience which you acquired in the novitiate. This will infallibly happen to you, if you do not attentively watch over yourself, and if you do not generously force yourself to preserve your fervor. If, before entering the religious state, you had the misery to offend God, watch over yourself in a very special manner. The devil will hover around you to regain his prey; he will take with him seven other devils more wicked than himself, and,—mark attentively !—if they enter into your heart and dwell there, your last state will be worse than the first. What a sorrow for Jesus Christ, what a triumph for hell, if you fall back into the slavery of sin!

Do all in your power to avoid this terrible evil : watch, pray, mortify yourself, flee, according to the counsel of the apostle, from even the appearance of evil. Beg every day from God, from the Blessed Virgin, and from your holy patrons, the grace of perseverance.

Keep up your fervor, observe faithfully your rules, and the devil will be powerless against you: all his attacks will turn to your advantage and his shame. You wish God to give you special graces in order to avoid sin? Force yourself to inspire a lively horror of it in those who are intrusted to you; make use of all the means in your power to preserve their innocence, and the Lord will reward you a hundred-fold for what you shall do for them. This zeal, which will cover your past sins, will prevent you from falling into them in future.

Have the salutary custom of praying for those who are tempted. God will measure to you in the same way as you shall have measured to others.

If, in spite of the desire to be faithful, led away by the violence of the temptation, you have the misfortune to fall, do not be discouraged, but rise up immediately.

One is lost, if, after having committed a serious fault, he does not get up at once, and with courage.

Correspond Faithfully with Grace.

"We exhort you, that you receive not the grace of God in vain." (2 Cor. vi, 1.)

To lead you to follow the counsel of St. Paul, think, often, that nothing is more culpable and dangerous than the abuse of grace.

In fact, it is clear that the more a good is necessary, precious, and abundant, so much the abuses of it are more shameful and culpable. For, what is more necessary for salvation than the grace of God? What is more excellent, more precious, or more abundant? Ah! if you had known the gift of God, could you have abused it?

Nothing can be equal to the dignity of grace; it is, in an especial manner, the gift of God, the source of virtue, the principle of all merit; it is the support of weak nature, the sacred pledge of glory, and the precious seed of a blessed immortality; it is the price of the sufferings of a God, of the merits and blood of Jesus Christ himself, so that the graces which we receive, are, as it were, so many drops of that adorable blood which fall upon us. In your holy state of life you received the most abundant and precious aids; but do not forget that an account will be demanded, according to what each has received. Think frequently of the account which you must give of all the means of salvation which the goodness of God provides for you in religion! I have given you, God will say, lights, so vivid and so strong, to make known to you your duties: have you followed them? I have inspired you with so many good sentiments, that you might practise virtue, and to attach you entirely to me: have you corresponded with these?

You have heard my word so many times, you have made so many spiritual readings and meditations, and received so many good counsels and examples: have you profited by them?

You have made so many confessions: have they amended your life? You have received so many communions: have they sanctified you?

To resist, for a slight satisfaction, such abundant, continual, and efficacious graces, is it not to be wanting in fidelity to divine love? Is it not to be very guilty? Is it not to deserve the terrible reproach which Jesus Christ addressed to the ungrateful cities: "Wo unto thee, Corozain, wo unto thee, Bethsaida: for, if in Tyre and Sidon had been wrought the miracles that have been wrought in you, they had long ago done penance in sackcloth and ashes"? (Matt. xi, 21.)

But the abuse of grace is not only culpable, it is also very dangerous. By one of those terrible judgments which God inflicts in his wrath, the abuse of grace brings with it disgust, insensibility, and the withdrawal of grace. This is the punishment most terrible, most just, and the most ordinary, with which God strikes the unfaithful soul.

Moses, David, the prophets, all the sacred writers, often repeat threats like the following: "O Israel, I have called thee, and thou hast not heard me; I have invited thee, and thou hast rejected my invitation. My time is come, I will give thee up to the desires of thy heart; I will command the clouds that they rain no rain on thee, nor shed upon an ungrateful land their gentle dews. I will remove thy candlestick. The kingdom of heaven shall be taken away." We are often astonished that God bears so patiently with so many lukewarm and sinful people. "Ah," says St. Augustine, "God punishes them with a secret punishment, so much the more severe, as it is the more secret, by withdrawing from them his graces, and allowing them to sleep quietly in their tepidity and lethargy."

Prove your heart, and see if, on different occasions, you have not yourself experienced this withdrawal of divine grace. Reflect often on this important subject, and renew your sincere resolution to correspond with divine grace: 1, promptly, avoiding all delay; 2, generously, breaking through all obstacles; 3, continually, never relaxing in the good which you have undertaken.

Desire to Advance in Perfection.

Religious life, according to St. Thomas and all doctors of the Church, is a state in which one is exercised in becoming better, or in which one tends to perfection. Thus the religious ought to aspire to a more excellent degree of sanctity than that in which he is, and, consequently, he ought to labor unceasingly to correct his faults, to pass from bad to good, and from good to better.

He should have an ardent and constant desire of perfection; he should make this desire more lively and animated every day; he should apply himself to give it its full effect, and, consequently, he should not remain in the same state, but unceasingly advance from virtue to virtue. He ought never to be satisfied with himself, whatever his progress may be; nor say, I have done enough; but he should always act as if he had only just commenced, and so always have a hunger and thirst after justice. He should say with St. Paul: "I do not count myself to have apprehended. But one thing I do: forgetting the things that are behind, and stretching forth myself to those that are before, I press toward the mark, to the prize of the supernal vocation of God in Christ Jesus." (Phil. iii, 13, 14.)

Besides, for a religious not to tend toward perfection without ceasing, is to be wanting to a grave obligation of conscience. "It is a crime for a religious," says St. Jerome, "not to wish to become more perfect." "You are lost," says St. Augustine, speaking to a religious, "if, believing that you have done enough, you stop, without troubling yourself to think of greater plans for your spiritual advancement."

"Woe," says St. Bernard, "woe to those religious to whom their spiritual poverty is sufficient, and who are satisfied with their faults!"

What ought still more to animate you with a holy ardor, is the strict obligation of keeping yourself in the grace and friendship of God: and this is what you will never do, unless you labor, with all your might, to advance in virtue. All the doctors agree, that not to advance in the way of God is to go back. In vain you may wish to remain where you are, and not to become better nor worse : you wish what is impossible. We go up a stream, and, if we do not make continual efforts against the force of the current, we shall be carried back very soon ; far from resisting so much weakness, so many temptations and occasions which seduce us, we shall go back quickly, and so violently, that we shall in the end be thrown into the abyss of mortal sin and the gulf of perdition.

Aspire, then, unceasingly after perfection, and labor for it with more ardor, inasmuch as you have longer neglected to do so. Perfection is not the work of a day, but of a whole life : we go insensibly, step by step, but, what is most important, we should never turn aside. The desire which you should have for a perfect life, ought to be a sincere desire, which comes from the heart; an ardent desire, which animates all our feelings ; an efficacious desire, which shows itself in deeds ; a generous desire, which is capable of sacrifice ; and a constant desire, which never fails.

To excite in yourself this efficacious desire, often consider the inestimable advantages which perfection procures for you.

Through it, you enter into participation of the divine perfections, and, like true children, you bear on you the marks and likeness of your heavenly Father; through it, you subject your passions to the dominion of reason, you triumph over your enemies, you become truly happy, in so far as you can be in this miserable life; and, after having caused your happiness in this world, it is, besides, the foundation and measure of your glory for all eternity. Thus our Lord Jesus Christ has said: "Blessed are they that hunger and thirst after justice, for they shall have their fill." (Matt. v, 6.)

Faithful Observance of the Rule.

A novice is faithful and fervent; he esteems his vocation, he generously fulfils his duties, inasmuch as he loves and keeps the rule; he does not relax, or lose himself, except as far as he neglects it.

"The brethren," says the Ven. J. B. de la Salle, "should have a very particular esteem of everything which relates to regularity, however unimportant it may seem to be, considering it, in their regard, as the first means of sanctification; for it is in this that they find the principal aid to enable them to observe the commandments of God, and the chief support against all the attacks of the devil, however violent they may be; and because God attaches his graces especially to them."

Elsewhere he says: "We do not receive graces in a community, except in proportion to the fidelity with which we keep the rules; we make more progress in perfection by the faithful observance of the rules, than by any other way."

The rules are, undoubtedly, the most meritorious, the surest and easiest, of all the penances and practices of self-denial. The most meritorious, because they do not allow the religious to belong to himself, and place him in the happy necessity of fulfilling constantly the will of God; the surest, because, not being our own choice, and not exposing us to vainglory, they put us out of danger of illusion; the easiest, because, to be well observed, they only require, momentarily, a little good-will, and, consequently, place the most perfect abnegation within the reach of temperaments the most weak, and of characters the least energetic. It is in this sense that the B. John Berchmans was wont to say that the greatest of all mortifications was community life. St. Mary Magdalen of

Pazzi teaches the same doctrine. She says: "Make more of the state of obedience and of regular life than of the highest contemplation, because all the actions of religion are ordered and regulated by the Holy Spirit, and, in performing them, you are certain of doing the will of God; but you have not this advantage in your particular exercises, however good and holy they may be." If you understood well the full value of this delightful assurance of doing the will of God, you would set no bounds to your love for your rules. In fact, of all the goods of heaven, is not this the one which is dearest to the saints, to the angels, and to our Lord? Can you doubt that our divine Saviour would be ready to leave heaven to go up again on the cross, if he knew that thus he would conform better to the will of God, his Father? Do you not know, on the other hand, that the uncertainty of what they ought to do to please God is one of the most painful trials of Christians who live in the world? You would, then, be very foolish, if, to sacrifice a caprice, you deprive yourself of the most valuable privilege of your state of life, and if you close up the most abundant of all the sources of merits which flow in the paradise of religious life.

Observe, therefore, your holy rules, if you would persevere in your vocation and receive all the helps which are necessary for the perfect fulfilment of its duties.

How different should I be from what I am if I had always been faithful to my rule, ought every bad and tepid religious to say!

Flee from the World: be Prudent in your Necessary Intercourse with Externs.

Intercourse with the world is dangerous for every religious, whatever his age or experience; but it is much more so for those who, like you, are just commencing the practice of virtue, and who are of an age when luxury, vanity, and pleasures have so much attraction. The Ven. J. B. de la Salle prescribes to his community, "as a matter of obligation and of precept, great reserve in regard to persons of the world, for fear of resuming their spirit, for which the devil gives to the majority of persons a natural inclination, which causes them to be attached to them, when they have frequent and free intercourse with them."

Thus he makes it an obligation for us to live separated from the world, to break all connections with it, and only to have those which are absolutely necessary; and even, in this case, he points out to us, in the smallest details, the wise precautions which we should take.

To preserve yourself from the dangers of the world, you ought:—

1. To guard your eyes with a scrupulous exactness. If you love vanity, you will soon love the world; but, if you guard your eyes, you will guard your soul. You must not only abstain from bad or dangerous looks, a prudent religious abstains even from such as are allowed, but which, not being necessary, only serve to satisfy curiosity. We must practise this custody of the eyes, in church, on the streets, in class, in the house, everywhere.

2. In your intercourse with the parents of the children, be always straightforward, but brief; never allow particular attentions or length in your conversations; distrust much every compliment or flattery, and every word which may be in the slightest degree doubtful. As soon as you feel that intercourse with a certain person makes a bad impression on you, tell the director, and put him in possession of everything.

3. Make no visit, and receive no one in the house, except for really good reason, and

with permission: in this case, even, neither say, nor let anything be said, which is not necessary; never discourse about worldly things: politics, news, accidents, family secrets, festivals or rejoicings, etc. Speak and behave with such prudence and reserve that people in the world may see, in every particular, that between you and them there is an unapproachable distance.

4. If you desire to keep your heart pure, and your soul in peace, in class you will be reserved toward the children in every difficulty; you will never allow any particular affection or natural attachment; you will avoid casting your eyes on those pupils whose figure, character, manners, deportment or dress, may please you; you will prudently refuse the too obvious marks of affection which they would give you. Experience will not be long in teaching you that we can count very little on the affection of children and their parents: those, who to-day seem most attached to you, will forget you as soon as they no longer need you. If you will preserve yourself in virtue, flee from the world, despise all that is in the world: have no intercourse with externs but what is absolutely necessary. "Know you not that the friendship of this world is the

enemy of God ? Whosoever, therefore, will be a friend of this world, becometh an enemy of God." (James iv, 4.)

Preserve and Increase the Interior Spirit.

With what force the Ven. de la Salle has recourse to this pressing obligation ! "What is most important, and to which more attention should be paid in a community, is that all who belong to it have the spirit which is peculiar to it. Let all the novices study to acquire it, and let all who are engaged in it make it their first care to preserve and increase it in themselves; for this is the spirit which should animate all their actions, and give the movement to all their conduct; and those who have it not, or who have lost it, ought to be looked upon, and look upon themselves, as dead members, because they are deprived of the life and grace of their state of life; and they ought to persuade themselves that it will be very difficult for them to keep themselves in the grace of God."

Do you wish to persevere in your holy state of life, to fulfil its duties, and to have its consolations and merits ? Then live by faith, develop in yourselves the interior spirit.

Trials, faults, the little fruit which we bring forth, the disgust of our vocation, and infidelity, only arise, because we are not interior enough, not sufficiently united with God, and because we do not sufficiently live by faith.

Repose of mind, joy, solid contentment, are only found in the interior world, in the kingdom of God, which is within us. The more we enter into it, the happier we shall be. Without this, we shall always be in trouble and difficulty, always discontented, always full of complaints and murmurings; and, if any temptation or hard trial come upon us, we shall not overcome it.

"If, in our employments," says Fr. Lallemant, "we practise external virtue without the interior, we are miserable, bearing the burden of exterior labor without enjoying the interior unction and sweetness: which is why we fall so often into serious faults; instead of making, by the help of recollection and prayer, our occupations, with less difficulty, disgust, and danger, and with more perfection for ourselves, more profit for our neighbor, and more glory for God."

Your principal study should be to make the interior spirit reign in you; that is to say, while acquitting yourselves of your obligations most conscientiously, you should not let yourselves be overcome by the prejudices, difficulties, and hardships, which you meet with. If your intention is right, if you only propose to yourselves to accomplish the will of God, you will do your best in all things, since you will remain tranquil and resigned to everything which may happen to you, even to what is most painful. You will especially guard yourselves from rushing, of your own accord, into distracting employments, which are only adapted to make you lose the interior spirit, or to flattering your vanity, by giving you relief in the eyes of men.

Make yourself very familiar with the practice of ejaculatory prayers, of elevations of the soul to God, of looking into yourself to find out what is defective in your actions, and to examine the motives with which you act.

Nothing is more consoling, or more fitted to support you in good, than these pious practices. You should have acquired them in the novitiate; you must preserve them with care, if you would secure your perseverance, and lead a holy life, fruitful in the ways of salvation.

Perform all your Actions with Great Purity of Intention.

The intention is the object and choice of the end for which we should act. Purity of intention consists in forgetting ourselves, disengaging ourselves from all self-interest, and in having God alone in view, his good pleasure, his love, and his glory.

According to St. Augustine, we must consider two things in every action,—the body and the soul: the body, which is, as it were, the foundation of the action; the soul, which is the motive of it. If there is only the body, there is nothing for God: it is the intention and motive alone which can promote his glory. Without the intention, the action is but a shell, a phantom, and a body without soul and life: God cannot accept it, and his glory in it amounts to nothing.

There is no action, however small and trivial it may be, which, raised by purity of intention and motive, does not become precious and great before God, and is not a thousand times more valuable than all the treasures of the world.

On the other hand, the grandest works,— those which are apparently most holy and meritorious,—if they are performed with a faulty intention, are vile and despicable in the sight of God, and become for us even a cause of condemnation.

"It is to do nothing," says St. Bernard, "if we do anything except for God alone. It is to imitate the fool who puts pieces of gold into a sack full of holes, or who goes to draw water in a sieve."

Hence let us understand the blindness and misery of losing the merit of all our actions, for want of directing and purifying them by a right intention and a holy motive.

"By your works thus purified and directed," says St. Augustine, "you can merit heaven, and prepare brilliant crowns for eternity. Why, then, alas! are you losing such great goods? Why do you deprive yourselves of such important gains?"

To act with a right and pure intention, is not as easy as we think. In fact, it is not enough that we have commenced our labor with a *Hail Mary*, or, *Come, Holy Spirit*, nor even to have repeated with our lips, *My God, I study for the love of thee*, etc. In truth, how many times does not our divine Master reply to us in secret, without our wishing to hear: "No, it is not for me that you are laboring"! And this is but too often very clear; for, if we were really studying because

God wills us, why do we follow our own caprices, instead of the direction of obedience? We pretend that we labor only to please God: whence comes it, then, that we are troubled when our works do not please men? What does this matter to us, if we have only sought the will of the Lord? Is not our end gained as soon as our task has been done as well as our means allowed?

Now, do you wish to know what is the best means of preserving purity of intention? It is to take care to renew it frequently by formal acts; otherwise, it is in great danger of going astray, or of being destroyed. In fact, when the intention is only virtual, it grows weaker by degrees from its duration; and soon an enemy rises up: I mean, some bad motive, which destroys it. Try, then, to restore it to its original energy. Do this, especially when beginning those actions which are more full of dangers, because they flatter your natural inclinations : and this is the case, not only in recreation and meals, but also in certain studies and occupations which are according to your taste. Then it happens that we are led away, or, which comes almost to the same thing, we only think of the intention mechanically and formally; and thus self-love devours that which might have been so meritorious. Ah! for pity's sake, do not allow this loss of your goods and treasures!

In order that your attention may be more perfect, accustom yourself to associate Jesus Christ our Lord with everything that you do. You will find in this a special encouragement, and a firm support in what is contrary to nature.

What good you will accomplish! How many merits will you heap up, if you persevere, all your life, in the practice of purity of intention!

Make your Spiritual Exercises with Great Care.

We never see a novice grow lax while he carefully performs his spiritual exercises, and keeps firmly to his pious practices; but the moment there is any break in them, by indifference or weakness, the seed of relaxation begins to grow. The ruling principle of your whole life, the foundation of all your actions, must be to give the first place to your spiritual exercises, the object of which is your own advancement; and never to be guilty, in this respect, of the least negligence, for any reason whatsoever. The constant observance of this rule will preserve you in virtue, and will make you more and more perfect.

On the contrary, however slightly you neglect it, you will immediately perceive the injury which is done to your soul. A fatal experience teaches that, when we deviate from the path of virtue, it is always in consequence of some neglect in our spiritual exercises : " My heart is withered, because I forgot to eat my bread." (Ps. ci, 5.)

" If, from a reason of piety, or for the good of a brother, we sometimes interrupt our ordinary exercises, it is an omission which it is easy to repair afterward. But if, through disgust or negligence, we get into a habit of leaving them, it is a serious fault, of which we shall feel the injury." ("Imitation of Christ.")

Watch yourself seriously on this point, especially at the beginning. Establish good habits in this matter, when you enter into the community. Apply yourself to your exercises as much as in the novitiate, since they are more necessary for you, as you have more needs and less help. Be punctual at the commencement of all, perform them with exemplary application ; never isolate yourself from the rest ; do not allow yourself a useless word or a voluntary levity during so valuable a time. In extraordinary circumstances and unavoidable interruptions, make them up as faithfully as possible.

There are certain employments, in which a person is often prevented from making the spiritual exercises with the rest: it would, therefore, be very prudent never to take upon yourself to judge if the reasons for being absent are good or not. The necessity of obtaining permission will make the absences more rare, because they would be caused only for good reasons, and not imaginary ones: which frequently happens, when we take counsel only with ourselves.

The loss of every religious who neglects his spiritual exercises, is inevitable. When, in order to omit or shorten them, we are satisfied with the slightest pretext, when we have no zeal for them, and scarcely any will to please God, we have already fallen into a sad relaxation.

We repeat to you, relying on the teachings of all the masters of the spiritual life, and the lessons of experience : If you wish to preserve the fruits of the novitiate, and to persevere in your vocation, perform your spiritual exercises well; perform all your exercises perfectly.

PERSEVERANCE.

Make your Meditation well.

The saints and masters of the spiritual life look upon prayer as an infallible remedy for all the ills of the soul, as the school of all virtues, and as the principal means of advancing in perfection, and securing perseverance and salvation.

Prayer is the buckler of the religious, and particularly of the young religious; without it, he is only a weak soldier without arms, in the midst of enemies who are devoted to his destruction.

If you relax in prayer, your whole conduct and all your actions will be tinctured with it.

"Ask the religious, who looks behind him after having put his hand to the plough, why he was once so pious, so humble, so obedient, so modest, and so mortified, so content when warned and reprehended for his faults, so indifferent as to his employment, so happy in his holy and sublime vocation; ask him why he had so much delicacy of conscience, so much simplicity in his manifestations of conscience, and in his intercourse with his director, and so much zeal in instructing his pupils in the truths of salvation, and he will reply: 'It is because at that time

I used to make my meditation well.' As streams no longer flow when the source is dried up, and as fire is extinguished when there is no more fuel, so grace no longer comes down from heaven, when, far from cultivating it through the means which God has given us to obtain it, we despise and reject them, and make use of them no longer.

"Let us apply ourselves, therefore, seriously to prayer; let us remember that it is the first and most essential of our daily duties; that it does us honor, that it puts us in relation with the best of all masters, and the tenderest of fathers; that it is by this channel that we receive the most abundant graces to confirm us in our state of life, the most ready help to overcome our difficulties, and the most mighty strength to support us in all our troubles."

But, that prayer may produce these happy results, make it well; prepare the subject of it with care; overcome repugnance, dryness, and disgust, and, above all, make practical resolutions, and seek for the means of securing their execution.

To excite you to perform well the holy exercise of prayer, often meditate on the beautiful words of St. Vincent of Paul: "Do not expect great things from one who does not know how to converse with God. There is nothing more useful or more necessary than mental prayer; we must bring all our care to make it well, and to conceive a real love for it."

Make the Particular Examen, and that of the Evening, with Great Care.

You have learned, during your novitiate, the theory of the particular examen; you know that, in this exercise, we set ourselves to consider, every day, not the general state of our conscience, but the state of it as it relates especially to a particular vice or virtue, or to one of our exercises or duties, in order that we may see, on these different points, our infidelities or our faults, and may labor seriously to correct our faults, and perfect our virtues.

All spiritual exercises may concur very effectively in the destruction of our vices, especially when we make this the particular intention; but, in the particular examen, this special intention is the foundation and substance of it, since its direct and essential end is the destruction of faults, and the acquiring of virtues. This is the reason why all the masters of spiritual life urgently recommend the particular examen as one of the most powerful means of sanctification which can be made use of.

Make, then, a firm resolution to perform this exercise well, and hold it for a certainty that it will procure you immense advantages. But take care; you will not go far, without being tempted to give it up, or to make it formally and with negligence. As the particular examen requires attention, that we may know ourselves, watchfulness in following it up, and generosity in overcoming ourselves, there are few persons who make it with good effect. This is why there are so few who make progress in the way of perfection.

Never forget that all those who neglect the particular examen remain stationary, or even go back in their path; while those who discharge this duty with persevering application, make, every day, new progress in virtue. In order that the case of the latter may be yours, follow with fidelity the following counsels:—

Choose the subject of your examen, in union with your director; above all, attack those faults which offend or scandalize your neighbor; then attack your ruling passion. Do not change the subject of your examen, until you have destroyed, or decidedly weakened, the fault which you have first attacked, unless it should be more profitable to combat another for a time, and then return to the charge against the first with a new zeal.

Mark down, every day, the results of your examen, with great exactness: if you are not faithful to this point, you will draw but little fruit from this exercise. In order to sustain you against your natural inconstancy, you can make it your duty to present to your director, every week, or, at least, once a month, the paper on which you mark the results of your examen.

Do not pride yourself on your success; and, also, do not be discouraged at the seeming uselessness of your efforts.

Impose upon yourself, every day, some mortifications in regard to the virtue which you propose to acquire, or the fault which you propose to overcome.

At public penance, and at manifestation of conscience, make known, with exactness and simplicity, the faults which have any relation to the subject of your particular examen.

In your prayers and good works, in your communions and exercises, propose to yourself the destruction of your ruling defect, as the end.

Meditate frequently on the truths relating to your particular examen.

During the time of the examen, follow the five points according to the method of St. Ignatius; occupy yourself, less in reading, than in giving an exact account of your faults, and in exciting yourself to contrition and firm resolutions.

God grant that you may generously follow these counsels! In return for your fidelity, we promise you abundant consolations, the destruction of the faults which give you pain, and the acquisition of virtues, which, without this useful practice, would always remain more or less imperfect.

Never fail, at your night prayers, to make your examination of conscience; make it with exactness and severity. It is a powerful means to prevent tepidity and negligence, to avoid relapsing into sin, and to rise out of it more speedily, if you have the misfortune to fall into it. Without this examen, we commit a multitude of faults, which, being neglected, may lead to relaxation and infidelity. Thus, say the saints, the conscience of one who only examines himself too negligently, is like a vine which falls in a fallow ground, and is soon covered with thorns and briers, because it has not been tilled. By this exercise, on the contrary, we make the examination for ordinary confessions easy, we amend our lives, we prevent the surprise of a bad death, and of the judgments of God. To say all, in one word, according to St. Gregory: To make daily our examen well, is a mark of the elect; to neglect it, on the contrary, is the mark of the reprobate.

If you wish to draw fruit from your examen, it must be religious, exact, and sorrowful:—

1. Religious; that is to say, you ought to make it in the presence of God himself, and in the brightness of his light, the better to discover the weakness of your heart.

2. Exact; that is, you ought to pass in review before you, your thoughts, desires, words, actions, and omissions; to give an account of the manner in which you have fulfilled your duties toward God, your neighbor, and yourself; to see if you have been faithful to your morning resolutions, if you have fallen into your predominant fault, and if you could appear before God with confidence, etc.

3. Sorrowful; that is, accompanied with a lively contrition at the sight of the faults which you have committed, and with a firm purpose of avoiding them in future, even

from the next day, and not to fall into the too common mistake of many pious persons, who only occupy themselves in finding out their faults, without thinking of being sorry for them.

If, during the time allotted to the evening examen, you were distracted; or if you could not examine yourself sufficiently, or excite yourself to contrition, you must make up for this defect, at the foot of your bed, before retiring to rest. Attach the greatest importance to this practice.

Essential observation.—If, by a misfortune, of which the very thought only makes you tremble, you acknowledge yourself guilty of a grievous sin, while making your examen, make a sincere resolution to confess it as soon as possible, and excite yourself to perfect contrition, until you have attained the sweet confidence that God has pardoned you.

One must be very blind and hardened to go to rest, with mortal sin in the soul. It would be a thousand times better to go to sleep with a viper in your bosom, or on the brink of a frightful precipice; for, to go to sleep at enmity with God is to expose yourself to the danger of waking up in the abyss of hell. What a frightful evil! Who can think of it without shuddering?

Go to Confession Regularly, and with Holy Dispositions.

If you are faithful in confessing, usually, once a week, and if you have suitable dispositions, you will not only not go back, but you will daily make fresh progress in virtue.

To arrive at this happy result, practise well the teaching which you have received in the novitiate on this important subject.

On confession days, prepare yourself in the morning, during meditation, so that you may not be prevented from doing so properly, when the time shall have come. Make use, from time to time, of a formula of examination. Without this precaution, you expose yourself to the danger of forgetting faults, of which it is very important to accuse yourself.

Without the express order of your confessor, nor without very good reasons, do not dispense with weekly confession. To act otherwise would be to deprive yourself of many graces; and you would derive from the sacrament of penance only a part of the aids which it offers you.

In fact, in confession, you receive, not only the absolution of your sins, but also great strength to avoid them in future, great light to discern them, and an abundant grace to repair the losses which they have caused; you practise the virtues of faith, hope, humility, obedience, justice, strength, and simplicity, and, by this act of confession alone, you exercise more virtues than in the majority of others.

Besides, it is a matter of experience that the fulness of the good and practical effects of a well-made confession last seldom longer than a week. At the end of this time, we do not commit grievous faults, it is true; but we generally notice a certain decrease of fervor in our prayers, and a little less restraint in our words and in the mortification of the senses; we commit a multitude of infidelities, which we would not have allowed on the day of confession; and this little relaxation goes on always increasing, until a new confession comes to restore to the soul the energy which it has lost. When this new confession is a long time coming, the evil is aggravated, the delicacy of the conscience is dulled, habits take root, and perfection is never attained.

A weekly confession, well-made, is necessary, if you sincerely wish to be ranked among good religious.

Go to confession more frequently, if the necessities of your soul require it. Have recourse immediately to this efficacious remedy, as soon as you have fallen into any fault which disquiets you.

It is to this fidelity that many are indebted for their perseverance.

Fervently Approach Holy Communion.

One of the most holy and useful customs which you should have acquired in the novitiate, is that of fervently approaching the holy table.

On leaving the novitiate, you will not find the same external helps; the thought of holy communion will be less frequently recalled to your mind. It is necessary, therefore, in consequence, to make more personal efforts not to approach the holy table without serious preparation. Be carefully on your guard against routine, levity, and tepidity.

It would be impossible not to preserve your fervor, and increase it, if you had a tender devotion toward the Holy Eucharist, and if you brought the requisite dispositions to the reception of this sacrament.

"Our life," says Fr. Lallemant, "ought to be only a preparation and thanksgiving for holy communion. Who can express what our Lord would work in our souls, if we were well prepared to receive him? A soul which is well disposed receives, in a fervent communion, a favor incomparably greater than that of all the visions and revelations which all the saints together have ever had. But, as we are without devotion, tepid, and negligent, this sacrament works no more upon our soul than on the walls of the church in which it reposes, because it does not find in us dispositions proper for the effects of grace. We suffer immense loss for want of knowing the grace which we have in holy communion, and of preparing for it. Our folly in this is deplorable."

A very good sign of fervor in the service of God is, doubtless, to love to go to holy communion, ardently to desire it, to be happy when the time arrives, to make frequent extraordinary communions when circumstances allow; but do not forget that you must prefer fervent and well-prepared communions to those which are frequent. St. Aloysius of Gonzaga and St. Stanislaus communicated seldomer than many pious persons of our day; but we know how they made up for this most profitably, by the excellence of their preparations and thanksgivings.

Consecrate, at least, the day before communion to the remote preparation; and let all your actions be done, to this end, with more perfection than usual. Think of it in your visits to the Blessed Sacrament, and in your pious practices, and excite in yourself holy desires by frequent ejaculatory prayers. If a few slight faults escape you, use all your efforts to blot them out by contrition.* In the case of a failure somewhat more serious, consult your confessor.

It is right that the thanksgiving should be continued through the whole day. For this end, you will offer all your principal actions: you will consecrate yourself to this, in your visits to the Blessed Sacrament, and you will take great care that this holy day be distinguished from ordinary days by union with our Lord, and by the purity of your intentions. This is the great means of proving the fruits of your communions; and we judge far better from the diligence which we bring to them, than from the sensible pleasure which we experience in them.

---

* A master of the spiritual life said: " We often derive more fruit from communion when we approach with some slight fault, because, in that case, the humility and shame with which the soul is penetrated, draw down upon us the merciful look of our Lord; whereas, when we go to communion, satisfied with ourselves, there are grounds for fearing that God may not be so satisfied with us."

Have Great Openness of Conscience.

Your perseverance is secured, if you have sufficient candor to manifest yourself well, and sufficient docility and courage to put in practice the advice which shall be given you.

At no period of life is it more necessary to make a good manifestation of conscience, than after leaving the novitiate.

Let this exercise be a principal business; prepare for it in advance; lay open fully your difficulties, troubles, and temptations; only be afraid of one thing: not to be sufficiently known to your director. Father Lallemant used often to say to his novices: "You ought, during your whole life, to lay open your conscience to your director, with great candor and simplicity, hiding nothing from him of the movements of your hearts, in such a way that, if it were possible, you would have your whole interior in your hands to show it to him." Weak and inexperienced as you are, what great need you have of a guide, consoler, and support! By listening to the repugnance of nature, and the illusions of self love, do not deprive yourself of so valuable a help. How many young persons have been lost, because, when they were in community, they did not have the same sincerity as they had in the novitiate!

"Many," says the Ven. J. B. de la Salle, "lose the spirit and grace of their vocation, because they had not a perfect candor of heart to their superiors. Yet, without the observance of this essential rule, it is impossible to be free from the bad consequences which may follow from the temptations with which the devil attacks those who are called to community life. Those who guide themselves, and who do not give themselves up to the direction of their superiors, will fall, like leaves from the tree, because, says St. Dorotheus, they are in league with the devil and the enemies of their own salvation."

If you wish, therefore, to persevere, make your manifestation well; do not always wait for the appointed time to speak of your interior with your spiritual director; go to him every time that the necessities of your soul make it a duty for you.

But, in order that manifestation may be possible, easy, and profitable, it is necessary that you should be closely united with your director. Do all that you can to attain this result.

Avoid, therefore, all prejudice which the devil may put in your mind against him, avoid all judgments contrary to his, avoid every interior murmur, and, still more, every external murmuring against anything which he may have prescribed for you. Combat your antipathies, overcome the sadness and vexation which nature may suggest to you, on any matter which he may command. Do not allow false reasoning, pretexts, or disguises, to lure you from what he desires; for all this is nothing else than the destruction of obedience, peace, spiritual joy, and union of hearts: in a word, it is the plague of a community.

Be faithful and affectionate to your director. This feeling, which is closely allied with respect, will produce in you that openness of heart which will become as salutary to you as it is agreeable.

Practise Modesty, Recollection, and Silence.

If you wish sincerely to live for God, and to persevere in your holy dispositions, love recollection, and keep faithfully the rules of modesty and silence.

Recall to your mind, frequently, how much, during your novitiate, the esteem of these virtues has been insisted upon; how much, their necessity in religious life; and on the special love, to which those who devote themselves to teaching should consecrate themselves.

Beware of believing that these instructions are only for novices: you ought to follow them all your life.

Every time you see your superiors, you should remember these things. At every annual retreat, at every visit to the Blessed Sacrament, in a number of circumstances, you cannot fail to recall this point: Is it not enough for you to understand their importance in order to make you practise them?

Keep silence, live in recollection, as much as you possibly can: on this condition, you will preserve peace of soul, fervor, and union with God.

Without a continual and strict watch over your senses, you expose yourselves inevitably to the danger of soon losing all that you have gathered together, with great toil, during your first years of probation.

"As nature," says Rodriguez, "does not produce trees without leaves or bark, nor fruits without skin, and as it creates nothing, without, at the same time, producing certain accessories to adorn and preserve it; so grace, acting in a similar way, though still more perfectly, does not fail to plant virtue in a soul, and make it blossom, without surrounding it with all the accessories of which we are speaking. It is the bark, the skin, which covers this heavenly fruit. Deprive yourself of this preserver and protector, and you will soon see it wither and grow rotten."

Recollection and silence, so necessary to keep you in virtue, are also necessary, if you would do any good to your brethren, and to the children who may be intrusted to you.

Nothing is so apt to scandalize, and give a bad opinion of a religious, as dissipation and the want of custody of the eyes; nothing, consequently, exposes you so much to the danger of losing that confidence which you need in order to do good.

"Exterior modesty, silence, and recollection," says St. Vincent of Paul, "are preaching without words. These virtues are, as it were, the characters which distinguish the true servants of God from men who are the slaves of sense; and, as they take their rise from interior grace, they necessarily produce wonderful effects on those who practise, and on those who witness, them."

Preserve the Spirit of Piety.

"Godliness is profitable to all things, having promise of the life that now is, and of that which is to come." (1 Tim. iv, 8.)

A devout religious is remarkable for exactness in all his spiritual exercises; his prayers show a person deeply penetrated with what he says; the frequentation of the sacraments is always for him an important matter; all which has any relation to religion is dear to him, and finds him always full of respect; he is known by the way in which he takes holy water, makes the sign of the cross, kisses a statue or picture, or makes an act of adoration; his demeanor in church is a subject of edification for all who see him; the practice of elevations of the heart to God, and of ejaculatory prayers, is so usual with him, that his whole day is, so to speak, a continual prayer.

Without piety, you can neither acquire nor preserve the spirit of your vocation.

Without piety, you will not have the consolations, nor fulfil the duties, of your state of life.

Without piety, you will not do the good to which you are called.

Without piety, you will not persevere in your holy state of life.

We may say of piety what Solomon says of wisdom: "All things come together with it."

Piety draws upon us the love of men, and the blessing of God. It makes us amiable, devoted, humble, charitable, and resigned to everything.

A pious religious is like the tree spoken of by the prophet, which, planted by the streams of running water, brings forth fruit in due season.

"Piety," says St. Francis of Sales, "is the perfection of charity. If charity is milk, it is the cream; if it is a plant, piety is the flower; if it is a precious stone, piety is the brilliant; if it is an excellent balm, piety is the odor. It is a perfume of sweetness, which strengthens men, and rejoices the angels."

A pious novice is a treasure to the community to which he is sent; he carries everywhere the sweet savor of Jesus Christ; he is a source of edification for his brethren, his pupils, and his neighbor; he is especially the consolation and hope of his superiors.

How happy is the young religious who has received from God the spirit and gift of prayer! What a treasure in his poverty! What resources in his tribulations! What protection in danger! What an infallible remedy for all his ills! What an abundant source of consolation and peace in his hardest trials!

Piety is the first of all blessings. Always place it, in your estimation, above talents and exterior qualifications, since, according to Bossuet, it is all man. But do not forget that, if you do not preserve it with care, if you do not nourish it unceasingly, it will not be long before it is extinguished. You must nourish it by the fervent frequentation of the sacraments, by application to your spiritual exercises, by the generous practice of mortification, by the care of keeping recollection and silence, by walking in the holy presence of God, and by animating your actions with motives of faith; in a word, by fidelity to all the practices which you should have learned in the novitiate.

Generously Practise Mortification.

"They that are Christ's, have crucified their flesh, with the vices and concupiscences." (Eph. v, 24.)

"Perfection," says St. Francis of Sales, "is not acquired by crossing the arms: it is procured by laboring courageously in subduing yourself, and by living, not according to your inclinations and passions, but according to reason, order, and obedience."

Without mortification, we cannot be happy: "Happiness is found, not by following the inclinations, but by combating with them." ("Imitation.") "Woe," says St. Vincent of Paul, "to him who flees from the cross, because he will find heavier ones, which will overwhelm him."

Without mortification, we can do no good. It is by the cross that Jesus Christ saved the world: it is by mortification that you can render all your labors efficacious. "Unless the grain of wheat, falling into the ground, die, itself remaineth alone. But, if it die, it bringeth forth much fruit." (John, xii, 24, 25.)

"A religious who is truly mortified, produces more fruit," says St. Vincent of Paul, "than a large number of others who are too tender with themselves, and too anxious to seek their own ease."

If you wish to atone for past faults, to guard yourself against new falls, to draw down upon yourself the grace of God, to comfort the souls in purgatory, and to prepare for yourself a glorious reward, imitate the example of Jesus Christ and of his saints: mortify yourself.

But in what should you do this? In everything, and at all times. Especially, mortify your predominant passion, fight against the faults of your character, repress the sallies of humor, and generously cut off everything which will be an obstacle to the fulfilment of your duties.

A mortified religious is never dainty, delicate, or hard to please, as regards food; he is always ready to make the little sacrifices which duty requires: to rise at the sound of the bell, to bear patiently weaknesses, fatigues, and privations. This costs but little. He is piously ingenious in imposing upon himself a multitude of little privations, which have the double advantage of being known only to God, and, consequently, of not opening the door to self-love; and which, besides, often become the source of the most precious merits. Nothing is more suitable to subdue nature, and to make us independent of the slavery of the senses.

As the Ven. J. B. de la Salle says: "Offer to God, from time to time, an act of mortification, by making yourself insensibly dead to self; be a continual sacrifice which you may make use of to pay your duty to God, and which rises up to him as an incense of sweet savor."

If mortification frightens you, think of Jesus Christ, of your sins, and of heaven; trust in God, and, by his grace, the flesh and the world will be subject to you. Fervor of spirit will make you love what nature abhors.

An illustrious penitent was asked how he could bear the greatest austerities. "Ah! do you not see," said he, "that I am supported by the strength of Him for whom I suffer?" It will be so with you in the midst of your pains.

If you die with Him, you will also live with Him; if you share in the pain, you will share in the glory. If, on the other hand, you do not mortify yourself, you will inevitably perish: "If you live according to the flesh, you shall die. But if by the spirit you mortify the deeds of the flesh, you shall live." (Rom. viii, 13.)

In proportion as you are mortified or not, you will obtain the grace of perseverance, or you will fall into infidelity: life or eternal death, heaven or hell, is your portion. Choose which it shall be.

Keep in the Sentiments of Humility which you have Gained in the Novitiate.

Do not forget the instructions which you have received in the novitiate on the dangers of pride, and on the necessity of humility.

How many young religious are lost, because they have not put them in practice!

Do you wish to be happy, to do good, to draw down abundant graces upon yourself, to work in a way which is always meritorious, and to be loved by God and man? Then, be humble.

Pride, on the contrary, is the source of all our troubles, the origin of all our faults; it corrupts all the good that we do, makes us slaves of the devil, disposes us to shameful falls, deprives God of his glory, and ourselves of eternal happiness,—and all, for an empty vapor.

St. Gregory has written a sentence which ought to make all those who are not humble tremble. He says: "The most evident sign of reprobation is pride."

Fight against this dangerous vice with all the energy of your soul. Be watchful over yourself; have no voluntary thought or word which is founded in pride. You are about to begin an action with a proud intention:

do not do it; if, however, it is good, and of obligation, purify your intention, so that you may not lose the merit of it.

Make it a rule never to speak of yourself, whether for good or evil, when you can absolutely avoid it.

Do not imitate those little minds who think they make themselves admired by an affected walk, demeanor, or manner.

Know how to bear a contradiction, or even a humiliation, without a frown. The true poison of pride is humiliation: to have a horror of humiliation, and to think that you are humble, is the height of illusion. "A great humility always suffers willingly great contempt; a little humility only bears a slight contempt. If, then, I cannot bear contempt, I have not even the first degree of humility; and, inasmuch as I am void of humility, so much I am full of pride." (Fr. Huby.)

If pride is your ruling inclination, make it the subject of your particular examen for a long time. Never make a meditation, a visit to the Blessed Sacrament, a communion, or any other spiritual exercise, without earnestly begging of God, through the intercession of Mary, the destruction of your pride, and the acquiring of humility. Never forget you will have no real piety—you will be dry, cowardly, easily discouraged, presumptuous, rash, foolishly vain, irascible, headstrong, arrogant, ambitious, jealous, tenacious in your opinions, and predisposed to all vices, if you are proud; whereas, if you are truly humble, you will be inundated with consolations, and loaded with heavenly gifts. May God grant you the grace to become so!

Carefully Practise Religious Poverty.

In the novitiate, you have learned to value holy poverty, and you have conceived an entirely filial affection for this mother of religion,—would it be right for you to be less zealous in practising it, when you are in the community?

A religious is obliged to take care of those things of which he has the use: they belong to God in quite a special manner; and it would be a crying shame that he should use them worse than those which he would have had in the world. Be attentive, then, and diligent in using them: this is what the poor do. When one of your garments is torn, have it mended as soon as possible, that the rent may not become worse; and, if there are stains upon it, clean them without delay: this is the way to make it last longer. Take care not to spoil or break anything; direct your attention, too, to the common property of the house, so as to preserve it from injury if you can. Never allow yourself to give, receive, or lend, anything, without permission.

If you have the management of money belonging to your class, never dispose of a cent, of your own accord; keep your accounts with perfect exactness; be watchful, so that nothing be lost.

It is to act against holy poverty, when you have superfluities for your use, when you collect books together without real cause, and when you keep them longer than you require. Good religious take great care to direct their attention frequently to these points. Be on your guard against being inordinately attached to any thing. Receive with gratitude, and as an alms given to the poor, what may be given to you for food, for use, or for study; know how, also, to take a refusal.

When anything is wanting, and discretion does not permit you to speak of it, do not be satisfied with bearing this privation with patience; love it, and say with joy: "I begin to perceive that I am really one of the poor of Jesus Christ: so far I have had only the name."

Regulate your Conduct by Obedience, and Give yourself up to the Will of your Superiors without Reserve.

Meditate often on the words of the Ven. de la Salle: "There is no virtue so necessary for you as obedience, since it is essential to your state of life. It alone is able to sustain you in it; and, even though you may have all other virtues without it, they would be only externally evident, because it is obedience which, in a member of a community, gives to other virtues the form which is peculiar to them." These counsels are for the whole life, and not for the novitiate only.

Perfect yourself, then, every day in the practice of obedience; see God always, and God alone, in the person of your superiors; subject, not only your will to them, but also your judgment; obey always with eagerness; never dishonor your obedience by murmurs or replies.

Be faithful in leaving your work or exercise, when obedience calls you elsewhere: if you do not, tell me for whom you are acting so. It is not for God; for you cannot have the intention of pleasing him, when you are doing what he forbids you at the very moment: it is not he whom you have in view. Far, then, from deserving a reward, that word which you are writing, that sentence which you are reading, etc., will be rather worthy of punishment.

Obey, then, in the spirit of faith, without knowing the reasons: that is not your business. If you knew them, perhaps you would find them so excellent, that there would be no longer any faith in obedience.

Do the holy angels, when they execute the orders of the Lord with so much zeal and alacrity, presume to understand the thoughts of the Most High? And you!—The wonderful secrets of his providence are sometimes hidden under an order the most simple in appearance, and the salvation of many souls may depend on its execution.

Obedience of faith, without forethought as to success: whatever be the employment, accept it. If it goes well, it is a blessing; if ill, a humiliation: a certain profit in either event.

Be always, in the hands of your director, like a pliant tool in the hands of the mechanic.

Never find reason for refusing a position or employment: to withdraw yourself from obedience, as the author of the "Imitation" says, withdraws you from grace.

It is necessary that subjects should be careful not to trouble the thoughts of superiors. The more their action is free, the more we can hope for the blessing of God, whatever may be their reason, even when it is not formal. A certain bent of their mind toward one side rather than the other, hides the will of God, and sometimes even great designs of his providence.

Never lose sight of this counsel of the loving St. Francis of Sales : "Never ask for anything, never refuse anything, but put yourself in the hands of Providence, without entertaining any desire, except to wish what God wishes of you."

"Superiors," says F. Valuy very happily, "to govern wisely, have three things, which you have not : views for the general good, the knowledge of subjects and of positions, and the special graces which God grants to the ministers of his authority."

You will never have more consolation and success than in the employments which you accept, without having sought for them ; even in those which are contrary to your natural inclination.

Every day's experience proves this truth. Besides, it is not at the beginning of your career that you will be most exposed to fail in conformity to the will of your superiors; but the rule which we give is fixed and unchangeable : it embraces all the circumstances of time, places, and persons.

We entreat you earnestly to adopt it for your whole life, and never to go astray from it : "Abandon yourself, my son," we say to you with the author of the "Imitation," "and you will find Jesus Christ. The more perfect and sincere your abnegation, the more pleasing you will be to God, and the more you will gain from it."

Excel in the Practice of Chastity.

Religious should excel in the practice of this angelical virtue.

Chastity should adorn and embalm their soul.

Being, in a special manner, the temples of God, the sanctuaries of the Holy Ghost, the well-beloved of Jesus Christ, and approaching so often to the holy table, they ought to flee from the shadow of evil ; they should lead the life of an angel in a mortal body. It is especially to them that the Lord says : "Be ye holy, for I am holy." (Lev. xi, 44.)

"Let it be your principal study, in regard to your exterior," says the Venerable de la

Salle, "to make your chastity outshine all your other virtues."

"It is not enough for you to excel in the virtue of purity," we say to you with St. Vincent of Paul, "but you ought to use all your endeavors, and behave yourself in such a manner, so that no one may have occasion to conceive, in your regard, the least suspicion of the contrary vice ; for this suspicion, even if it had a very slight foundation, would be more hurtful to your ho y duties than all the other crimes which might be imputed to you."

Love, then, with all your heart, this inestimable chastity, which is the happiness of the soul, and the rest from all passions; love this incomparable virtue, which is the admiration of heaven and earth, and which raises man even to the dignity of God. Love this virtue, which must necessarily be preserved, or regained by penance, if we wish to be in the number of the elect. Oh ! sacrifice everything, even your life, if need be, rather than that it should suffer the slightest stain.

Means of Preserving Chastity.

As the devil knows that, if you remain perfectly chaste, you will infallibly become a holy religious, he will make incredible efforts to cast you into the filth of the vice of impurity.

To render his attacks useless, flee from all the occasions which holy chastity fears.

Detest idleness, which is the sworn enemy of this virtue.

Be perfectly modest, especially in your looks. The eyes are the gates of the heart; it is through them that the impure spirit gains entrance into the soul. How many temptations are provoked by imprudence and curiosity!

At the first approach of an improper thought or a dangerous remembrance, act as if a spark had fallen in your heart: cast it from you.

Practise some acts of mortification, not at long intervals and in moments of fervor, but habitually and in a regular manner.

Be strict with regard to your reading; never read anything which is, in the least degree, tainted with levity.

Cultivate humility: "The unclean spirit," says St. Bernard, "cannot resist the spirit of humility."

Have a dread of particular friendships. Seek for none, and do not yield to those in which you see any sign of them.

Never have any preference for those children to whom you may feel yourself attracted by the good manners or natural qualities which they possess.

Have a tender and special devotion to the Blessed Virgin: intrust to her the care of your heart.

Recite frequently the prayer, *O my Queen!* etc.

Approach the sacraments according to rule, and with fervor. "The devil," says St. John Damascene, "cannot fight against a person who has his lips purpled with the blood of Jesus Christ."

Endeavor to preserve a childlike innocence, pray for those who are tempted, and God will give you the graces which are necessary to keep you pure.

Devote yourself to piety with all the power of your soul. As long as you are thoroughly pious, you will be invulnerable. Never take away one link from the chain of your spiritual exercises: the impure spirit respects a pious soul; he trembles at the sight of it, and dares not come near. But when it grows careless and loses its fervor, he takes courage; and, if it continues to relax. he most certainly will make it his victim. How many young people have learned this by sad experience!

It sometimes happens to most holy souls that they suffer very painful attacks. The great apostle was not free from them, and God inspired him to tell us so for our consolation. If you are put to this proof, do not be astonished or frightened, and do not be discouraged. As long as these things cause horror to you, it is a sign that the will has nothing to do with them, and that the heart remains perfectly unscathed. You will not have to answer for the perverseness of your enemy, who suggested them to you; and all that he will gain himself will be to increase your merits and strengthen your virtue.

In circumstances so delicate, know how to have immediate recourse to God, but with calmness and confidence: perhaps the Lord permits your temptations, in order to oblige you to think often of him.

It is a great consolation for a poor soul, harassed by these impure phantoms, not to be exposed to them willingly: it can address our Lord with more confidence, that it may be delivered from them. But it would not be the same if it had to fear this reply: "Is it not your fault? Why did you seek the danger?"

Strive to Acquire Fraternal Charity.

"Put ye on, therefore, as the elect of God, holy and beloved, the bowels of mercy, benignity, humility, modesty, patience: bearing with one another, and forgiving one another, if any have a complaint against another: even as the Lord hath forgiven you, so do you also. But, above all these things, have charity, which is the bond of perfection." (Col. iii, 12-14.)

You will be a good religious, if you are a religious who is eminently charitable. You ought, therefore, to show yourself zealous in causing this divine virtue to flourish in the midst of your brethren, which St. Paul, according to the example of Jesus Christ, has recommended in so earnest a way. To help you, it will suffice for us to point out briefly what it demands on the one hand; and, on the other, what it forbids.

What fraternal charity demands, above all things, are humble and docile hearts; from this source all the rest spring forth: disinterestedness, cordiality, mutual esteem and confidence, delicate foresight, the most efficient eagerness in doing service to others, and, when it is necessary, bearing with the faults of one another, and the readiest and most complete forgetfulness of mutual wrongs.

That which dries up charity, above all, is egotism, with its icy distinction of *mine* and *thine;* the details of which are pretension and haughtiness, jealousy, impatience, rudeness and bitter words; besides indelicacy and independence, susceptibility and rancor, antipathies and coldness, or exclusive friendships; the spirit of curiosity and the affectation of cleverness; taciturn and tricky ways, or excessive gossiping; suspicion and distrust, indiscreet relations; and the inclination to criticism, disputes, raillery, and mockery of our brethren.

If you feel in you a certain amount of sharpness and bitterness against your neighbor, as soon as he is cold or opposed to you, be sure, by this, that you are predisposed to a thousand faults which charity condemns. Destroy this spirit, or, at least, root out the poisonous plants which infect it, and replace your coldness and bitterness with gentleness, benevolence, and cordiality, and even with tenderness, to everybody.

Be master of your tongue, and govern it so well, that you never allow it intentionally to be used at the expense of your neighbor. Regard nothing as slight, in the matter of charity. Make a scruple of the least raillery, and refrain from uttering any word which would displease yourself, if it were said of you.

If you have been subject to be manifestly wanting in charity to your brothers, as, for example, by speaking to them, or by acting toward them in a hasty or haughty manner, etc., impose upon yourself the obligation of begging their pardon, and do not forget to do this as often as you may have forgotten yourself. By this means you will make reparation for your bad example, and you will more easily correct this great fault.

Never speak ill of others, however slightly. From slight evil-speaking it is easy to pass to more serious: and the habit of evil-speaking being formed by little and little, we no longer see evil, where the eye of God sees very much.

Insist strongly on this point of charity, in your confessions, manifestations, meditations, and examens.

Be hard upon yourself in this important matter; let nothing pass by; punish yourself for the least breach of it, and do not lay down your arms until you have given to your charity those ravishing characters which St. Paul assigns to it. (See 1 Cor. xiii.)

Truly Love the Community.

Father Alvarez, of the Society of Jesus, often said to his novices: "Walk in the perfection of your congregation, in spirit, in heart, and in practice: in spirit, by conceiving a high esteem for it, and by considering it as a counsel and guidance coming from God; in heart, by loving it tenderly, as the happiest and most important thing in the world; in practice, by obliging yourself to make all the actions of your life conformable to it."

We address to you the same language: Yes, honor and love the community, and force yourself to be useful to it. These are sacred obligations, which ought to be very dear to you.

The community is the society which has received you into its bosom; the family, which has admitted you among its members; the society or family, to which you belong in an altogether special manner, and which has procured, and procures you still, such great spiritual advantages.

Justice and gratitude impose it upon you as a duty, to honor, to love, and to be useful to it, as much as you are able.

To discharge these obligations:—

Conduct yourself in a truly religious and edifying manner, at all times.

Venerate your worthy Founder.

Speak only well of the community.

Reject, at the very beginning, every thought which would be unfavorable to it.

Esteem everything which is special and peculiar to the community.

Do all that depends on you to maintain it in regular observance.

Take great interest in its preservation and prosperity.

Put yourself in a condition to do much good in it.

Pray for it often, and always with fervor.

Lend a generous concurrence to your superiors.

Help your brothers as much as possible.

Encourage the vocations of subjects who may really do well in it.

Watch over yourself, so as to exercise no influence, except in the way of regularity and charity.

These are the means by which you may discharge the duties which you owe to the community, and which will give it reason to rejoice that you have been admitted among its members.

Have Great Zeal for the Salvation of Souls.

One of the principal effects of the presence of grace in a soul is to inspire it with an ardent zeal for the salvation of our neighbor. In fact, how can we truly love our neighbor, how can we love him as ourselves, if we do not desire the salvation of this other self, and not contribute, as much as lies in us, to make him work it out? How can we love God, and not desire that he should be known, served, loved, and glorified, as much as he deserves to be, by all men? How can we not be penetrated with grief at seeing him offended and outraged by his ungrateful children? How can we love our Lord Jesus Christ, and not have our hearts filled with bitterness at seeing this good Master despised in his benefits, and a multitude of souls rushing to damnation, notwithstanding all that he has done to open heaven to them?

Whoever knows the value of souls, which have cost Jesus Christ all his divine blood— of one single soul, which is worth more than all existing worlds, and of which the loss is a greater misfortune than the destruction of all the earthly and heavenly bodies,—whoever is penetrated with these truths will not be astonished at the zeal which the saints have shown for the salvation of souls.

Walk in their footsteps, labor generously for the salvation of your pupils. What have not the Ven. de la Salle, and so many other religious who have devoted their lives to the education of youth, done for children? Imitate their devotedness and love, and, by your instructions, your good example, your sacrifices, and your prayers, contribute to the salvation of the greatest number of souls that you can!

What good will you not do, if you labor with constancy for your own sanctification, and for that of your neighbor?

How glorious will be the reward which you will merit by your labors!

Do not be satisfied with exercising the apostleship of teaching; practise, also, that which is more fruitful and easier, viz.: that of prayer and sacrifice.

Here are some practices which are suitable for nourishing your zeal, making it pleasing to God, and useful to your neighbor:—

Pray every day for the conversion of sinners, the perseverance of the just, and the spiritual progress of persons who are consecrated to God; in a word, pray for all the needs of the Church, and interest yourself in a special manner in the needs of the community.

Make your prayers and mortifications with the view of this apostolate.

Offer every day, with this intention, the actions which cost you most—the sum of your labors and good works.

How consoling will it be for you, at the last day, to see the good which you will have accomplished by your prayers and good works!

Be, then, a man of zeal; but of zeal, at once enlightened, constant, and generous.

"In this is my Father glorified, that ye bring forth very much fruit. Every branch in me that beareth not fruit, he will take away: and every one that beareth fruit, he will purge it, that it may bring forth more fruit." (John xv, 8, 2.)

Love Admonitions, and Profit by them.

A religious, and, particularly, a young religious, ought to love to know his faults, and correct them with generosity: and, for this purpose, he ought to take well the advice and admonitions which are given to him, and humbly to perform the penances which may be imposed on him for them. He should allow himself to be moulded, without opposing the least resistance; to be, in the hands of his superiors, like clay or iron in the hands of the workman. "Do you know," says St. Francis of Sales, "what a community is? It is an academy for correction, in which each soul ought to learn to let itself be treated, cut, and polished, so that, being well cut and polished, it may be joined, united, and fastened most closely to the will of God.

"It is an evident sign of perfection to wish to be corrected; it is the fruit of that humility which makes us know what we have need of.

"A community is a hospital of spiritually sick persons who wish to be cured, and who, to be so, are willing to undergo bleeding, the lancet, the probe, the iron, fire, and all the bitterness of remedies. We must either be cured or die; hence, since we do not wish to die spiritually, we wish to be cured; and, in order to be cured, we must suffer correction, and beg our physicians not to spare us. Sparing us may be very terrible to us, and hinder our cure."

He who has the misfortune to resist correction deprives himself of many graces. He offends God, scandalizes his brethren, and inflicts pain upon his superiors; he makes no progress in his employment, in the reformation of his character, and in the spiritual life.

"Now, all correction for the present, indeed, seemeth not to bring with it joy, but sorrow; but afterward it will yield to them that are exercised by it the most peaceable fruit of justice." (Heb. xii, 11.)

In order to receive corrections well, we must: 1. Think of their usefulness and of their necessity. 2. Be convinced thoroughly that they make us practise the most sublime virtues. 3. Recall the example of our Lord and of his saints. 4. Have regard to the edification which we owe to our brethren. 5. Think of the promises which we made, when we received the habit of religion. 6. We must remember our sins, and the punishments which we have deserved for them.

Do not be too much Afraid of Temptations.

"If we are tempted, it is a sign that God loves us," says the Holy Ghost. Those whom God has loved most, have been most exposed to temptation. "Because thou wast acceptable to God," said the angel to Tobias, "it was necessary that temptation should prove thee." These are consoling words, which you ought to take care to repeat whenever you feel your confidence shaken. Do not beg of God to deliver you from temptation;

beg rather the grace not to yield to it, and to make a holy use of it.

There is no artifice which the devil does not put in practice to hinder us from profiting by the trials of temptation, and to make use for our destruction of what, in the ways of Providence, had only been permitted for our justification, and in the way of salvation. This is why it is absolutely necessary for us to discern the wiles of the tempter, in order to resist him effectively, and to avoid the snares with which he seeks to surround us.

Now, the first of the artifices which he makes use of, is to frighten and trouble us; for this seducing spirit does not cause sin, except when the water is troubled. We cannot, therefore, too much possess our souls, and fortify them against the impressions of fear, in the most violent temptations: this is a powerful means of avoiding surprise, and of resisting the attacks of the enemy. Nothing disconcerts him so much as to see that we show him a firm and assured countenance; that we become more humble at all times, from the simple and quiet feeling of our weakness; that we are more experienced in our use of the power from on high, and that, finally, our weakness is strengthened by all that is done to overthrow it, as the reed is nourished by the very torrent which shakes it. "Temptations, whatever they may be, trouble you," says St. Francis of Sales, "because you think of them too much, and fear them too much. You are too sensible of them; for, as soon as you have the least thought contrary to your good resolutions, you imagine that all is ruined. Let the wind take its course: all the temptations which are possible, cannot bring a stain upon a soul which does not love them." Think at such a time that God is a good and tender father, and that he does not allow the devil to tempt men, except to render their merits more exalted, and their reward more brilliant. "Lastly," it is the same saint who is still speaking, "I was near the swarms of bees, and some of them settled on my face: I wished to move them away with my hand. 'No,' said a countryman, 'do not be afraid, do not touch them, and they will not sting you; if you touch them, they will wound you.' I believed him, and not one of them stung me. Believe me, too, do not fear temptations so much, do not touch them; they will not injure you. Go on, and do not trifle with them."

The longer the temptation, which is repugnant to you, lasts, the clearer it is that you have not consented to it. "It is a good sign," again says St. Francis of Sales, "that the enemy causes such a tempest, and so much noise around your will: it is a sign that it is not in your will. Dogs do not bark at the servants of the house, but at strangers: when the devil presses and torments a heart, it is a certain sign that it is a stranger to him, and does not belong to him." One does not besiege a fort which one holds in his power; and, inasmuch as the attack is obstinate, we may be assured that the besieged will sustain it. If you are attacked by the most violent temptations, even during your whole life, do not be disquieted; your merits will increase in proportion to your trials, and your crown will be more glorious. Be only firm in your resolutions to despise the efforts of the tempter.

Make a point of bearing with resignation the trial of temptations.

Hope humbly for the help of God, which will never fail you; if you persevere with courage in resisting, he will either deliver you from your enemies, or he will give you the grace to overcome them.

Know how to Profit by your Faults.

Everything should serve for your sanctification, even your faults. Form for yourself a conscience which is right and delicate, and which warns you of your faults, reproaches you with them, and which excites you to correct them. Nothing is more dangerous than a lax conscience, which leads you to neglect your little duties, and to keep no account of slight failures.

"But," says Fenelon, "we must also avoid reverting uselessly to our past faults, which embarrass the mind, and discourage the heart; we must humble ourselves for them, grieve for them, and leave them to take their course."

Above all things, after you have fallen, even when your falls have been serious, never give way to sadness, for "sadness has killed many, and there is no profit in it." (Ecclus. xxx, 25.)

This bad kind of sadness only comes from wounded self-love, and can only produce discouragement, and sometimes even despair.

Do not be astonished nor discouraged by your falls, whatever may be their nature. "Our imperfection," says St. Francis of Sales, "must accompany us even to our bier; we cannot walk without touching the ground. We must not lie down on it, or wallow in it; but we must not think of flying, for we are so little, that we have not any wings as yet. Though you should fall a hundred times a day, never allow yourself to be cast down by discouragement, which would be a still greater fault than all those into which you have fallen."

Remember that, when we take occasion to humble ourselves at the sight of our faults, we gain much by this loss; and the profit which we derive from it, in the contempt of ourselves, richly repairs the injury which might arise from our imperfections.

Faults which produce humility are more useful than good works which inspire vanity. Therefore, take great care not to fall; but, after a fall, encourage humility and repentance, and make a speedy and generous reparation. With these conditions, your faults will turn to your advantage; they will secure, instead of endangering, your perseverance.

What must be Done, so as not to be Discouraged at our Faults.

"If it happen," says the pious author of the "Peace of the Soul," "that you sin by deeds or words; that a certain event makes you angry; that a vain curiosity draws you from your exercises; that an immoderate joy transports you; that you have suspected your neighbor unjustly, or that you have fallen into a fault against which you had resolved to guard yourself, do not be discouraged for all that; do not lose time in recalling to your mind what is past, so as to afflict and disquiet yourself, imagining that you can never correct your faults, that you do not do what you ought in your exercises, and that, if you did so, you would not fall so often into this fault: for this is a want of confidence which you should avoid."

You must not stay to examine in minute detail the circumstances of your faults, to see if you gave full consent or not, or to find out how long it lasted; because this only serves to fill your mind with anxiety, before and after your confessions, as if you had not said what you ought to have said, nor said it in the way in which it should have been said.

You would not have all these troubles if you knew your natural weakness, and if you knew the way in which you ought to act with God after your falls. It is not with this distress and interior discouragement, which disquiets and casts down, but it is by an humble, sweet, and loving confidence in the goodness of your Father that you should have recourse to him, not only after slight faults, which are the effect of tepidity and indolence, but also after grave faults, which are committed through malice.

This is what many do not understand; for, instead of practising this great lesson of filial confidence in the goodness and mercy of God, they give way to such dejection, that they can scarcely entertain a good thought, and they lead a miserable and languishing life, because they persist in preferring their own imaginations to true and salutary doctrine.

Continue, through Life, the Struggle against your Faults which should have been Commenced in the Novitiate.

Far from lessening our watchfulness and generosity on entering the community, we ought to labor with more care to struggle against self, because faults find more occasions of developing themselves, and we have fewer means to overcome them. One single fault, even though it be light, if it is not overcome, is enough to jeopardize the future, to poison our very life, to make us fail in our duty, and to put the question of perseverance and salvation at stake.

Do you wish to know the reason of this? It is, says an illustrious bishop, because, since original sin, there is not an evil seed in us, however small and despicable it may be, which does not grow, if it be not fought against; and which does not succeed in seizing upon everything, in ruling everything, and in corrupting all: while, on the contrary, there is no good quality which has not a tendency to grow weak, if it be not encouraged, and if we do not strive to strengthen it.

This is why we must never neglect a good quality, a virtue, or a grace, however small it may seem to be: once neglected, it will perish. Hence so many vocations are lost, and so many futures are destroyed, because the first grace has been neglected.

To how many young persons has not the forgetfulness of this important truth been lamentable!

Profit by the experience of others, and prevent these miseries by serious and constant struggles against yourself.

Study seriously to know your faults well; fight against them with energy and with constancy, and, in order to succeed, make your particular examen well. You would be wonderfully deceived if you believed that the holy war, which you should have undertaken against your passions, was only to last for a time, and that, afterward, you could lay down your arms. "Believe me," says St. Bernard, "vices which are cut down, spring up again; when they are driven away, they return; when they are extinguished, they enkindle again, and, however much asleep they seem to be, they will awake. It is a little thing to cut them down once, they must be cut down often, and, if possible, always; because, if you speak the truth, you will always find something to cut down."

Do not grow weary of fighting against yourself, and do it until your last sigh, never complaining of the length of the war, and assured that the resistance of your enemies only gives you new occasions of gaining fresh merit; for, at each victory which you gain, the angels are preparing for you a new crown.

Struggle, especially, against your Ruling Fault, and Strive to Acquire the Opposite Virtue.

You ought certainly to have found out, during your novitiate, what is your ruling passion—that inordinate inclination, which is for you the most usual cause of temptations and faults. Could it be supposed, in fact, that you have employed a whole year in purifying your soul, without having made this important discovery? Perhaps you have discovered in yourself a disposition more inclined to idleness, to impatience, to pride, to love of your own ease, etc., and I presume, besides, that this inclination has been energetically attacked. Whatever may be the success which you have already attained, take care of believing that you have now nothing more to do than to fold your arms. Our ruling passion is generally seated in the very foundation of our being, and we must expect that it will give us proof of this throughout our whole life. But it is, above all, in this first passing from the novitiate to another order of things, that it is important to keep our eye upon it, and to make it the special object of spiritual combat. Therefore, having fully discovered your ruling fault, renew your struggle without delay, and apply yourself, in an altogether special manner, to the practice of the virtue which is opposed to it.

Doubtless, a religious ought not to neglect any of the virtues of his state of life; but there is one, however, among all the rest, which he should choose as his virtue of predilection, the practice of which should be the constant aim of his efforts, the habitual object of his desires, the most ordinary fruit of his meditations, and the grace which he will unceasingly beg of our Lord: it is the ruling fault which points out this virtue, because it should be the principal remedy for it. For you, for example, it will be humility, or obedience, or meekness, or conformity with the will of God, or the desire of pleasing him by purity of intention, or recollection, or the spirit of mortification, etc. Choose that which is suitable for you, that you may practise yourself in it diligently, and produce frequent acts of it, as well in your heart, as in your exterior, according to opportunity.

Do not Follow Bad Example.

There have been bad examples in heaven, in the earthly paradise, and in the college of the apostles; there may also be such in communities, even in those which are the most holy.

You may meet on your way with stumbling stones: you must expect them, and take precautions that they be not to you an occasion of failing: "Therefore, take unto you the armor of God, that you may be able to resist in the evil day, and to stand in all things perfect." (Eph. vi, 13.)

Put faithfully in practice this counsel of the pious author of the "Imitation:" "Profit by everything for your advancement; if good examples strike your eyes or ears, animate yourself to follow them. If, on the contrary, you see what is blameworthy, take care not to imitate them; and if this should sometimes happen, try to correct yourself as soon as possible."

"Always look upon the fault of another," according to Eucherius, "as a disgrace, and not as an example to follow."

If any one do evil, he will bear the punishment of it. Do not follow him in this any more than you would imitate him if he were to smear his face with mud, or to throw himself down a precipice.

Bad example is like a wind which breaks and tears down only weak trees, but which strengthens those which are well rooted in the ground.

Many are lost by bad example; others are sanctified by it. In which number will you be? "The Lord knoweth how to deliver the godly from temptation." (2 Pet. ii, 9.)

If you find any one whose example, words, or advice, may be dangerous, far from seeking his company, have no intercourse with him but that to which you are strictly obliged. On such an occasion have the courage to do your duty. You have heard or seen a certain thing which is evil, or which may have sad effects: warn your director of it, without troubling yourself about what will be thought of you, or of what may arise from it.

When a religious is, so to speak, the master of his duties, it is not to him that those who are irregular or discontented will address themselves; on the contrary, they avoid him, and he loses little by them.

Enter into the dispositions in which Father de la Colombière was when he said: "If the whole world were to rise up against me, to mock me, complain against me, or find fault with me, I wish to do everything which God commands me—everything with which he inspires me to his greater glory. I have promised this, and, with the assistance of his grace, I hope to keep my promise."

Application to Work.—Love of Study.

A father of the spiritual life said: "For one devil who tempts a religious who is well employed, there are a hundred who are thirsting for the destruction of an idle religious."

"Idleness," says St. Thomas, "is the hook with which the devil catches souls;" according to St. Chrysostom, it brings an inundation of evil thoughts. "The idle," says St. Bernard, with great force, "suck in crime."

On the other hand, labor, done in the sight of God, is the guardian of all religious virtues.

Therefore never be idle. Your time does not belong to you; it belongs to the community, to your pupils, to God; it is too precious for you to consent to lose even a single moment of it.

Happy is the young religious who loves labor, who flees from useless conversation and frivolous occupations! The accomplishment of all his duties, and perseverance in his state of life, will be easy to such an one.

On the other hand, he who does not know how to make a good use of his time, and who does not know how to employ himself constantly in a useful way, exposes himself to deplorable falls. How many persons have lost their virtue, through losing the love of labor! Their loss and their misery are explained by these words of Solomon: "I passed by the field of the slothful man, and by the vineyard of the foolish man; and behold! it was all filled with nettles, and thorns had covered the face thereof, and the stone wall was broken down." (Prov. xxiv, 30, 31.)

Therefore you will work: but what must be done in order to work usefully?

Apply yourself with all your strength, and with the interior spirit, to wnat is your duty.

If you are intrusted with a temporal employment, discharge it with the greatest care; neglect nothing; and dispose of your spare moments according to the will of your superior.

Your watchfulness and your care should extend to all the interests of the community; you are responsible for what you allow to be lost, for the useless expenses which you may cause, and also, to a certain point, for the health of the religious, if you endanger it by food which is badly prepared, or by your want of cleanliness.

If you are called to teaching, use all your efforts to instruct yourself: to neglect study would be to fail in one of your most important obligations.

Employ yourself, not in what pleases you, but in what is most useful to you

Before all things you must learn what is necessary for the welfare of your class.

Study, not to satisfy your natural inclinations, but to be able to procure more glory to God, and to be more useful to the community and to your pupils.

Have a method in your work; keep guard against curiosity, inconstancy, or precipitation.

If public lessons are given in the community, follow them as best you can; if you cannot do this, ask the director to give you a plan of study.

If you learn with great difficulty, do not be discouraged at the sight of the apparent uselessness of your efforts: one is rewarded, not according to the result, but according to the labor and purity of intention.

Pray often, in order to call down the blessing of God on your studies.

Consecrate to study all the time which is authorized by the rule and by obedience; never employ for it the time of your spiritual exercises, or that of your class. To study to the prejudice of your religious duties, or of your duties as a teacher, could only be very hurtful to your soul.

MONTHLY RETREAT.

WE earnestly recommend you to enter seriously into yourselves, one day in every month, in order to give an exact and detailed account of your conduct. Fidelity to this salutary practice, which will not hinder you from fulfilling any of your ordinary duties, will be eminently fitting to keep you in the fervor of the novitiate, and thus secure your perseverance.

Let us briefly show the necessity of this monthly retreat.

As religious life imposes so many and such extensive obligations, it is a rare and difficult thing to find that, after a certain time, one is not exposed to the danger of falling into a relaxed state. We make resolutions, and we use the means to preserve our fervor; in spite of this, our natural weakness is so great, that it is to be feared lest, by degrees, the influence of our weakness draw us away, or at least the fervor of charity grow cold. It is, then, important, nay, even absolutely necessary, to enter more seriously into ourselves, to see what, that is defective, may have entered into our conduct, and what might drag us still farther in the way of relaxation and tepidity; that is to say, we must rouse ourselves up from the sleep and drowsiness into which we may have fallen, and of which the consequences may be still more dangerous; in a word, we must put ourselves into that state in which we should wish to be, if we were soon to appear before God.

These are, doubtless, very pressing and effective reasons to inspire us with a salutary desire of this holy practice: thus it has become a custom in most religious communities; and souls which aspire to the perfection of their state fail not in making use of this help, to which our Lord generally attaches very precious graces.

Such are the reasons which should induce you to make a monthly retreat, whether it be to foresee your falls, or to raise you up from them, or, at least, to sustain you in good, and to advance you more and more in the way of justice.

Way to Make the Monthly Retreat.

Choose the day which you foresee will be most free, in order to consecrate it more especially to the great business of salvation. The first or last Sunday, the first or last

Thursday in the month, seem to be the days most suitable for this retreat. At least it is necessary that each one should himself fix, or get his director to appoint, the time which he ought to spend in it; without this, he would be exposed to the danger of putting it off from day to day, and the devil would not be wanting in pretexts to turn us away from a practice which is so well calculated to close to him entirely the door of our soul.

What must be Done on the Eve of the Retreat.

On the day before, in the evening, in order to prepare for this holy exercise, invoke the special assistance of the Blessed Virgin, of your patron, your guardian angel, and of the saints for whom God has inspired greater devotion.

If you have the opportunity of going to confession, you can very profitably make a review of the faults committed during the last month. All these faults, collected under one point of view, are more capable of inspiring sorrow and compunction.

Make your spiritual reading in a book which is calculated especially to excite the will. As far as possible, have it selected beforehand, not to lose time in looking or searching about for it.

You might read the preparatory meditation for the monthly retreat, which is on page 125.

It would be very useful to perform some act of mortification during the meal, in order to draw down the blessing of God upon your retreat. You should oblige yourself, during recreation, to be more recollected than usual. Evening prayers should be said with more attention and fervor.

When retiring to rest, receive spiritually the holy viaticum, and, especially, extreme unction, which consists in making the sign of the cross on those parts of the body which are anointed in the sick, saying, at the same time, the prayer, "By the sign of the cross," etc.

Go to sleep as if you were dying, reciting the ejaculatory prayers, "Jesus, Mary, and Joseph, I give you," etc.

Contemplate, with the eyes of the soul, your corpse lying upon the bed of death.

Imagine yourself appearing before the judgment-seat of Jesus Christ.*

---

*Valuable material for Meditations for the Monthly Retreat will be found in Vercruysse's Meditations, vol. i, page 556 and following.

What is to be Done on the Day of the Retreat.

On rising, consider that this day has been given to you to settle your accounts with God; and banish carefully every thought which is capable of distracting or dissipating you.

As soon as you are dressed, make, if possible, a visit to the Blessed Sacrament, to offer yourself to Jesus Christ, to beg his blessing, and to ask him to grant you the grace of drawing abundant fruits from this monthly recollection.

Make your meditation with all possible fervor and attention: you might, during this time, make the preparation for death, particularly if you have not been able to make it the evening before.

Assist at holy Mass, as if you were assisting at it for the last time, and receive holy communion as viaticum, and with the dispositions in which you would desire to be on your death-bed. During your thanksgiving, beg of our Lord the assistance you need in order to correct your faults, to advance in perfection, and to spend the following month well.

Say your Rosary with more fervor than usual, in order to put your monthly retreat under the protection of the Blessed Virgin.

In a word, perform, in the spirit of renovation, not only your pious exercises, but all the actions of the day, even the most ordinary.

The review, strictly so called, may be made during the spiritual reading: for this end, make use of the method of examen, pointed out afterward, page 129.

It would be useful to write down briefly the result, so as to be able to compare it with that of the retreats which preceded or will follow it.

Choose the subject of the particular examen for the next month, whether it be a virtue to be specially practised, or a vice to be especially fought against.

Foresee the principal difficulties which you may meet with during the month.

If the monthly recollection be made on a Sunday, assist with great fervor at the benediction of the Blessed Sacrament, in order to merit more and more the grace of true amendment. Offer to our Lord the resolutions which you have made, and pray to him to make you faithful to them.

End this holy day with some prayers of thanksgiving.

Preparatory Meditation for the Monthly Retreat

You can read very profitably the following pages, during the spiritual reading on the eve of the retreat, and make it afterward the subject of your meditation.

Recall to your mind the healing of the blind man at Jericho. He fell at the feet of Jesus, who said to him: "What would you that I should do unto you?" "Rabboni, grant that I may see," answers the blind man. "Go," answered our Saviour, "thy faith hath made thee whole." (Mark x, 51, 52.) Listen to Jesus Christ asking you the same question, and answer him like the blind man: "Lord, that I may see. Show me clearly, in this retreat, what displeases thee in me, and what thou expectest from me."

Pray God to produce in you the dispositions in which he wishes you to be, to fulfil all the views of his mercy, on this day of grace which he deigns to grant you.

1st. *Disposition of desire.*—Happy Jerusalem, if she had known the value of the visit which the Saviour made to her in that day, which he wished still to grant her, and to call her day! "In this thy day!" (Luke, xix, 42.) Happy art thou, my soul, if thou dost appreciate the gift of God! What losses may be repaired! With what pleasure can the holy employment of this simple day of recollection fill thee! Have I, at least, the desire to know myself? Have I not some fear of allowing an importunate and accusing light to penetrate into my conscience? If I have this desire, I ought seriously to examine at what point is the work of my sanctification. Have I advanced on the way to heaven? Have I not fallen back toward hell? I ought to demand of myself an account of the exercises which I have made, of the graces which have been lavished upon me, of the sacraments which I have received, and of the duties which I have had to fulfil. What victories have I gained over myself, the devil, and the world? Would the judgment of God, if it were to come suddenly on me, cause me more alarm than it would have done at the time of my last retreat?

2d. *Disposition of confidence.*—God presents himself to me, and offers me his help. If I was alone with my sins, my weakness, then, indeed, I should have a reason to be discouraged; but, with God, I can do all things. His grace is stronger than all hell united. It is ready to spread itself over me in abundance: I have only to ask for it. God loves me always, whatever my infidelities may be: I have a proof of this in the invitation which he gives me to come and repose myself near him, in silence and retreat. I hear him saying to me: "Come into solitude, and I will speak to thy heart." O my soul! Jesus calls thee; he says to thee besides, as he did to the first companions of his labors: "Come apart into a desert place, and rest a little." (Mark vi, 31.) What goodness! what a motive for confidence! Yes, in spite of the reproaches of my conscience, I can, and I ought to, hope for everything.

3d. *Disposition of generosity.*—God will be to me, in this retreat, what I shall be to him: "In what measure ye shall mete, it shall be measured to you again, and more shall be given to you." (Mark iv, 24.) "He who soweth sparingly, shall also reap sparingly; and he who soweth in blessings, shall also reap of blessings." (2 Cor. ix, 6.) If I give myself up fully to the grace of Jesus Christ, I shall draw down on me the blessings of his love. I wish, then, to abandon myself to my Saviour, like Saul, in the beginning of his conversion: "Lord, what wilt thou have me to do?" (Acts ix, 6.) I will say to him, with Samuel: "Speak, Lord, for thy servant heareth" (1 Kings iii, 10); and with holy King

David: "My heart is ready, O Lord, my heart is ready." (Ps. lvi, 8.) Finish this meditation, like the beginning, with the prayer: "Lord, that I may see what I am, what I ought to be; that I may see my soul as it is; that I may see my sins, my weaknesses, and thy mercies, which are still greater than my miseries." Or, if you like it better, make your own the prayer of the Royal Prophet: "Lord, grant me the understanding of thy commandments, and I shall live." (Ps. cxviii, 141.) O my God! grant me the understanding of my nothingness in presence of thy infinite greatness; the understanding of my duties, and of the reasons which urge me to discharge them faithfully, then I shall live by that faith which makes the just; my life will be worthy of thee, and of the great mission which thou hast confided to me: it will lead me to a happy and eternal life.

Material for Examination in the Monthly Retreat.

This is what may be the subject of your examination.

As it is extensive, it would be better to confine yourself to one part, and to penetrate it thoroughly, than to go too superficially through the matter:—

Duties of your Vocation, and the Care of Perfection.

What idea have I of my vocation? Have I strengthened it by the faithful discharge of my duties? Have I that esteem for it which it deserves, and that gratitude which it should inspire?

Is it my chief care to advance in perfection?

Are my dispositions, whether as regards my amendment or my advancement, the same as they were during my novitiate?

What progress have I made in the Christian and religious virtues?

Is my faith simple, lively, and active? Is my hope firm, without discouragement or presumption?

What is my love for God? Is there not in my heart some inordinate attachment to creatures? (Ambition and sensible friendships always produce this sad effect.)

Have I any zeal for the glory of God? Am I distressed at the outrages which he receives? Have I that delicacy of conscience which makes the good religious tremble, even at the mere appearance of evil? Have I not allowed myself many faults, under pretence that they were only venial? Have I not exposed myself to the danger of committing a grave fault?

How am I with regard to union with God, the remembrance of his presence, and conformity to his holy will?

Examine yourself more particularly on your efforts against your predominant passion, on your progress in the virtue which you proposed to acquire at your last retreat. See, especially, if, on account of the meagre results obtained, you have not given any admittance to discouragement into your soul.

As to poverty.—Have I received, taken, bought or borrowed anything without permission? Have I kept anything without being authorized to do so, anything to which I am inordinately attached, or anything which is superfluous, and little conformable to poverty? In all these cases, I must despoil myself without delay, and return to the exactitude of holy poverty. Do I take care of everything which I have the use of, as belonging to religion and to our Lord? Have I loved poverty as a mother, rejoicing that I wear its livery, and feel the effects of it? Does it not happen that I seek for that which is best, and leave what I reject to others?

As to chastity.—Am I faithful in watching over my thoughts, my heart, and my senses? Have I never allowed myself anything which has been to me an occasion of trouble? Am I faithful in having recourse to God at the first attacks of the enemy? Have I carefully fought against affections which are too natural? Have I avoided all familiarity, and every demonstration which is too friendly? How have I observed religious temperance? Do I do everything, as far as depends upon myself, to imitate the purity of the angels, by that of my body and soul?

As to obedience.—Is there, in my obedience, the spirit of faith and submission, as well of the will as of the judgment?

Do I see God in the person of my superiors? Have I listened to their voice as to that of God? (This disposition is the soul of obedience.) Do I do anything in secret? Have I obeyed promptly, at the first sign, at the first sound of the bell? Have I renounced a certain employment, a certain residence, at the first order, and even at the first hint, remembering that I must be indifferent to all things here below, except to the will of God, expressed by the will of my superiors?

Have I not allowed myself, on the contrary, to make reflections, pleasantries, criticisms, and murmurs, on the foundation or accessories of the orders, or on the person of my superiors; thus lessening, in my mind, and in the minds of others, the respect which is due to them?

Do I act frankly and with love in my relations to my superiors?

Am I faithful in keeping all my rules; or are there any of them which I have formally excluded from my obedience, or of which the violation has not become habitual? Have I, above all, esteemed and observed the rule of silence, which is so important for the community in general, and for myself in particular?

As to humility.—How do I stand as regards humility? Have I wounded it by boasting, susceptibility, self-sufficiency or haughtiness to my religious companions? Have I sought for esteem and praise, instead of loving to be forgotten and to be humbled? Have I acted from human respect? Have I not a good opinion of my talents and virtues?

Have I not a habit of speaking of, and of excusing, myself? Am I faithful in avowing my deficiencies with simplicity, in rendering an account of my conscience with that humility and childlike confidence which is so much in the spirit of the rule? Have I not been cast down when I do not succeed, and when I am blamed? Do I frequently make acts of humility?

As to fraternal charity.—I owe, to my brethren in religion, affection, esteem, and the most tender and cordial benevolence. I ought to encourage, with all my might, the union of hearts. Have I said or done anything which was contrary to these duties? Have I not given way to aversions, envy, malevolent interpretations, to resentment, disputes, and anger?

Have I driven far from me that low jealousy which is troubled at seeing the distinctions, the success, and even the virtues, of others?

I owe to my neighbor, whoever he may be, love, support, and forgiveness. Have I not allowed, in his regard, evil-speaking, indiscreet relations, calumnies, desires of vengeance, sallies of bad humor; in a word, everything which could give disedification, or produce disunion?

Have I taken care not to find fault with others, without having the right to do so, and not to criticise my brethren? Is my affection for them founded on the love of our Lord? Is it generous, effective, and universal; that is, without any exception?

Have I had a horror of those miserable particular friendships which scandalize our neighbor, divide the heart, and take it away from God, who wishes to possess it whole and entire? Have I thought of the sad consequences of scandal in a community, and of the necessity of giving good example?

As to mortification.—Is there in me any relaxation with regard to mortification? Have I fulfilled, in all their integrity, and according to their spirit, the rules which are contrary to the inclinations of nature? What efforts have I made to arrive at a perfect observance of religious modesty in my looks, in my demeanor, and in all my conduct? In difficult circumstances, have I not given signs of impatience, anger, or, at least, of distress? Have I fulfilled with courage and constancy the practices of mortification and penance which are customary in the community? Have I applied myself, especially, to interior mortification and abnegation? Have I made any efforts to reform my character? How have I received the trials sent by Providence? Have I labored to acquire a perfect conformity to the will of God? In fine, have I had the spirit of mortification? That is to say, knowing that sufferings are an excellent means to expiate my faults, to root out my vices, and to make me more like Jesus Christ, have I loved and desired them?

As to the exercises of piety.—How am I with

regard to my spiritual exercises? Do I make them with zeal and fidelity? Does it never happen that I neglect them through my own fault? When I have been obliged to put them off, have I not discharged them carelessly, or even have I not entirely forgotten them?

How does my meditation go on as to the choice and preparation of the subject, as to fidelity in following the method, as to resolutions and practical results? What is the cause of my distractions? Is it negligence in the immediate preparation, or is it habitual dissipation?

Do I carefully and profitably make the examens, especially the particular examen?

What is to be thought of my spiritual readings?

How do I assist at holy Mass?

Have I nothing to improve in my confessions and communions? What preparation do I make for them? What fruits do I derive from them?

Is my Rosary well said?

Have I made my account of conscience with exactness every week? Have I presented myself at a suitable time, when I have not been able to make it on the day and at the time appointed?

What is my docility in following the advice which I receive? Am I faithful in regarding my director as holding the place of Jesus Christ, and as having been given to me, on his part, to guide me according to the rule and spirit of the community?

How do I make my prayers during the day, and particularly the little ones before and after meals?

What graces should I not receive, if I were faithful in making well all my little prayers, and in being recollected in passing from one exercise to another!

As to the class.—I owe, to the souls intrusted to me, zeal, devotion, patience, and unvarying kindness: are these duties fulfilled?

How have I made the *catechism*, the *reflection?* Have I labored indefatigably for the salvation of my pupils? Have I always given them good example? Have I watched over them well? Have I prayed for them with the fervor which the desire of their happiness ought to inspire in me? "Have I made myself all to all," to gain them all to Jesus Christ? Is there any partiality or antipathy in my conduct? Have I not been too familiar or too harsh? Have I not punished from passion? Have I used all my efforts to obtain order? Has the time been always well employed? Have I done my best to inspire them with a horror of sin? What is their love for our Lord, the Blessed Virgin, and St. Joseph? Have I induced them to approach the sacraments frequently?

How do they say prayers in my class? What pious practices have I taught to my pupils?

Pause at this article, for there is no true piety without a faithful accomplishment of the particular duties which we ought to fulfil.

As to the care of ordinary actions, and the good use of time.—How do I perform my ordinary actions? Have I continually acted for God? Am I faithful in animating all my actions with motives of faith? Am I firmly persuaded that my perfection consists in performing well my ordinary actions? Have I well economized my time? Study is a duty for me: how have I fulfilled it, and with what intention? Is the order of my work subordinate to obedience?

Is there, in my actions, a religious diligence, or rather an inordinate eagerness, slowness, indolence, idleness, or loss of time?

How are my recreations and walks spent?

Have I a care to sanctify my meals, my sleep, and my bodily exercises?

You will place yourself upon your knees, to conclude this exercise with a fervent colloquy; in which, collecting the principal resolutions which you should have taken, you will beg of our Lord the pardon of your faults, of your tepidity, and of your negligences in his service; you will promise him to do your duty better during the month which you are beginning.

You can make use of the following act very profitably:—

Act of Renovation.

It is, then, necessary for me to think of a holy renovation, which may make me enter into the ways of perfection, to which thou hast called me, O my God! Here are the essential points, on which this holy renovation is absolutely necessary for me:—

Renovation in the exactness of all my spiritual duties; renovation in purity of intention; renovation in the preparation for the divine sacraments; renovation in an inviolable fidelity to grace; renovation in dependence and entire submission to superiors; renovation in the sentiment of gentleness and charity to all, without exception; renovation in the generous fulfilment of the duties of my employment; and renovation in the absolute detachment of my heart, which is made only for thee.

Here determine the particular resolutions which you wish to make.

These are my holy resolutions, O my God ! and this is the new plan of life which I am resolved to follow henceforth. I owe this holy renovation to the sanctity of the state which I have embraced; I owe it to gratitude, which the many graces I have received, inspire me with; I owe it to the sorrow and reparation which are required for the many faults which I have committed; I owe it to the edification of those persons with whom I have the happiness of living; I owe it to the care of my perfection, which I have so miserably neglected; I owe it to the spiritual good of those who are intrusted to me; I owe it, in fine, to the preparation for my eternity, into which I may, perhaps, enter before another renovation is allowed to me. I understand what I have to fear from my weakness, after the sad experience which I have had of it, after so many other renovations, after so many repeated promises: it will not be the same, I hope, after this one. Aid me, O my God! with fresh help of thy grace: with this help, I promise thee a more constant fidelity in fulfilling all my duties. I am going to labor, from this day forward, for this end. May 1 never go astray from it all my life! Most holy Virgin, St Joseph, my good guardian angel and my holy patrons! make me faithful to these resolutions; obtain for me the grace to be entirely renewed, in heart, in words, in deeds. (Hymn of the Blessed Sacrament at matins.)

Foresee, in concluding, the means which are most suited to secure your complete renovation. Put all your trust in God, and resume your course with ardor, without being cast down at the sight of misery, however deep it may be.

Preparation for Death.

This exercise essentially enters into the monthly retreat: if you foresee that you cannot make it in the evening, you can do so during the morning meditation.

Kneeling before your crucifix, imagine that your last hour has come, and that your good angel has come to say to you what the prophet said to Ezechias: "Your time has come; take order with thy house, for thou shalt die, and not live." (Isa. xxxviii, 1.)

First Reflection: What is Death?

Death is the passing from this life to eternal happiness or misery. It is the end of time, and of all temporal things; it is the entrance to a happy or a miserable eternity.

"I shall die!" that is to say, I shall leave all without exception: parents, friends, pupils; I shall bid eternal farewell to all things here below. I shall be separated from my brethren, and from every familiar association. I shall leave everything absolutely. Are there not some objects to which I am very much attached? I shall leave them, just as I shall leave everything else. O my soul! what impression does the thought of this universal abandonment make upon thee? It is inevitable. What folly, then, to be attached to what passes so quickly! How much trouble do we not give ourselves, in order to prepare ourselves regrets!

"I shall die!" that is to say, my body shall be separated from my soul, and from henceforth its presence will become disagreeable and painful to those even who have loved me most. It will be laid in the grave, where it will become the food of worms. Instead of flattering my flesh so much, which will soon be only corruption, what wisdom would it be to employ my health and strength in laboring ardently to promote the glory of God and the salvation of souls! When I shall be in the grave, shall I be thought much of among men? Oh! the dead are soon forgotten. The esteem of creatures is a very trifling thing.

"I shall die!" that is, I shall go into the house of my eternity. Time, the world, and all the things of time and of the world, will have disappeared like a shadow; eternity alone will remain. Oh, terrible moment! To appear before the judgment-seat of God, alone in his presence, to be examined about my whole life by this God who is sovereignly enlightened, sovereignly just, and the sovereign enemy of sin—and then without mercy! To go to hear from him whether the heaven of the good religious, or the hell of the wicked, is to be my lot for all eternity!

Second Reflection: When and How Shall I Die?

How much longer have I to live? I know nothing about it: people die at every age. Shall I have time to prepare for death? I do not know; I only know that many persons, even after a long sickness, die at a moment when they least expect it. Shall I receive the last sacraments, or shall I die without confession? I do not know: I may lose my speech suddenly. Besides, when one is sick, what is he capable of? What folly to count on this last moment, on which an eternity depends!

Third Reflection: Am I Ready to Die?

What are my present dispositions? Am I ready to leave everything? Am I prepared, above all, to appear before the judgment-seat of God, and to give him an account of all the benefits which I have received from his goodness, and of all the duties which have been intrusted to me? Is my conscience at ease? Is there nothing which troubles me with reference to my confessions, in the fulfilment of my duties? What imprudence to live in a state in which I would not wish to die!

After having dwelt, as long as you are able, on these powerful thoughts, and having made the resolutions which they ought to inspire, it will be good to recite piously the two following prayers, holding your crucifix in your hand:—

Act of Resignation to Death.

O Sovereign Master of life and death! O God, who, by an immutable decree, and in order to punish sin, hast appointed that all men shall die once! behold me humbly prostrate before thee, fully resigned to this law of thy justice.

I deplore, in the bitterness of my soul, all the sins which I have committed. I, rebellious sinner, have a thousand times deserved death; I accept it in expiation of so many faults; I accept it in obedience to thy adorable will; I accept it in union with the death of my Saviour. May I die, then, O my God! when, where, and in the manner, which thou mayst please to ordain. I will profit by the time which thy mercy deigns still to leave me, to detach myself from the world in which I have so short a time to live; to break all the bonds which attach me to this land of exile, and to prepare my soul for thy terrible judgments. I abandon myself, without reserve, into the hands of thy ever-fatherly providence. May thy will be done in everything and forever! Amen.

Prayer to Beg the Grace of a Happy Death.

Prostrate before the throne of thy adorable Majesty, I come to beg of thee, O my God! the last and most important of all graces, the grace of a happy death! Whatever bad use I may have made of the life which thou hast given me, grant me the grace to end it well, and to die in thy love.

May I die, like the holy patriarchs, leaving this vale of tears without regret, in order to go and enjoy eternal rest in my true country!

May I die, like the blessed St. Joseph, in the arms of Jesus and Mary, repeating those sweet names, which I hope to bless during all eternity!

May I die, like the Blessed Virgin, inflamed with the purest love, and burning with the desire of being united to the only object of my affections!

May I die, like Jesus on the cross, in the most lively sentiments of hatred for sin, of love for my heavenly Father, and of resignation in the midst of my sufferings!

Eternal Father, into thy hands I commend my spirit: have mercy on me!

Jesus, who art dead through love of me, grant me the grace to die in thy love!

Holy Mary, Mother of God, pray for me, poor sinner, now and at the hour of my death!

Angel of heaven, faithful guardian of my soul; great saints, whom God has given me for protectors, do not abandon me at the hour of my death!

Holy Joseph, by thy intercession, obtain for me the grace to die the death of the just! Amen.

A hundred days' indulgence is attached to each of the following invocations, every time they are said (Pius VII, April 28, 1807.)

Jesus, Mary, Joseph, I give you my heart, my soul, and my life!

Jesus, Mary, Joseph, assist me in my last agony!

Jesus, Mary, Joseph, grant that I may expire in your company!

OF OUR EMPLOYMENT.

Dispositions in which we Ought to be, in Regard to Different Employments.

You must be perfectly indifferent as to everything which obedience may order for you; that is, you should ask for nothing, refuse nothing, and desire nothing. We do not know, sufficiently, what is suitable to us according to God, to dare even to determine for ourselves; we should often find trouble where we had sought for peace, and also temptations dangerous to our salvation. It is especially in regard to our employments that we should practise obedience to superiors, because in that it is of more importance than in anything else that we should be led by Providence.

" He, O Lord !" says St. Augustine, "deserves to be called thy servant who does not ask thee to command him what pleases him, but who simply aims to desire what thou commandest."

No one can say that he has a true conformity to the will of God, if he does not abandon himself entirely into his hands that he may do with him what he pleases, at the time and in the way that he wills, without any opposition or reserve on his part.

One of the principal motives which should lead you to accept with joy the duties, whatever they may be, which obedience may call upon you to fulfil, is to know that the will of your superiors is the will of God. This ought, in fact, to be a great happiness and consolation for a religious, in the accomplishment of all the duties which obedience prescribes, viz.: to have a certainty that he is doing the will of his divine Master.

Nothing satisfies the needs of our soul better than this thought: God wills that I should do such a thing at this time. We ought to desire nothing more, for there is nothing preferable to the accomplishment of the divine will. If you practise these maxims, you will never be disquieted by what it shall please superiors to command you; it will be of little consequence to you whether you have an exalted or humble employment. You will always be contented, always resigned, and always blessed by God.

The Esteem and Love which we Should Have for Obscure Employments.

It is a sublime act of virtue and perfection to accept for love of God, with a joyful heart, the most obscure offices, and be far from aspiring to those which are more important and honorable. "A man," says Rodriguez, "who is bound for life to the service of a great lord, and who should consent to fulfil, if need be, the lowest offices, would certainly give a greater proof of zeal and devotedness than he who would only serve him, on condition that he should be employed in high offices, which bear, in a way, their reward with them; and the more fitness such a servant had for more exalted duties, the more his master would become acquainted with the humility of his feelings and conduct." It is the same in religious life: if you wish to serve God only in high offices, you do not make a great effort, and you do not give him a very signal mark of your devotion and zeal; but, if you are ready, on the contrary, to serve him all your life in the humblest duties, which are most opposed to the inherent pride of your nature, and which are most repugnant to your delicacy of sense, be certain that you offer him a far more brilliant testimony of your love; and the more talents he may have given you, the more pleasing will your humility be to him. This consideration alone should be sufficient to make you wish to occupy the lowest place in the house of God, where, moreover, there is none which is to be despised. There are no small offices about the king, says a popular adage; by whatever title, in fact, we serve our sovereign, we always derive honor from it: how much more glorious, then, will it be to serve the King of kings, even in the humblest offices, since to serve him is to reign!

To Desire a High Office, even with the Idea of doing Good in it, is often an Illusion.

Those who aspire to high offices, with the thought that they will do much good in them, are wonderfully deceived, if they think that these desires arise from a disinterested zeal for the love of God, and the salvation of their neighbor. Such ideas show, for the most part, a secret ambition, and betray the desire which we have of being esteemed and thought much of, and of living at our ease; they prove, in a word, that the employment which we wish to obtain, is either more honorable, or more conformable to our taste, than that in which obedience places us. If you were in the world, and entirely free from all dependence, you could, at choice, leave one occupation for another, with the object of making yourself more useful to your neighbor. It is not the same in religious life: we cannot give up one office for another. "It is necessary," says Rodriguez, "that all the wheels of our organization should work at the same time, that each should do his part; and, if you do that which is high, another must do that which is low." If you were truly humble, you would desire to see the important offices given to another rather than to yourself, because you would be convinced that that other would prove himself more worthy of this honor than yourself, and would be less exposed to give way to pride in it.

Another advantage of humble offices is, that we expose ourselves far less than others to temptations of vainglory. In high functions we practise charity, but we run a great risk in giving way to the seductions of vanity and self-love; while, in humble employments, we practise at once charity and humility, especially the latter, which, in a certain sense, finds in them its natural element. This consideration alone should be sufficient, not only to keep you from every ambitious thought, but, still more, to make you fear, as a great misfortune, to find yourself raised above your brethren.

Of the Manner of Discharging our Duties.

We must discharge the duties of our office with assiduity, doing everything with care and exactness, and neglecting nothing which is prescribed.

"Be assured," says the Ven. de la Salle, "that you will never work out your salvation better, and that you will never attain so much perfection, as in fulfilling well the duties of your state of life, provided that you do so in the sight of God."

However unimportant your duties may be, it is always the will of God that you should perform them well: the least trifles become as high as heaven itself, when they are considered in this point of view

One cannot discharge badly any duty whatsoever, or neglect it, without the members of the community suffering from it.

We should discharge our duties with dependence, conforming ourselves, in all things, to the will of our superiors, disposing of nothing without permission, and doing everything in the place, time, and manner, prescribed. To act thus is to give to everything that which constitutes the precious merit of obedience. On the contrary, to be guided by ourselves is to act in an entirely human and worldly manner; to draw upon ourselves unpleasantness, to commit many faults, to lose great graces, and to expose ourselves, it may be, to be seriously wounded in our conscience.

It is not enough to discharge our duties with application and dependence: they must also, and above all, be discharged in a spirit of faith.

To fill an office from entirely human and natural motives, from taste, vanity, self-love, or human respect, would be to separate ourselves from the spirit of God, and to lose the merit of all our actions: it would not be to act as a Christian, far less like a religious.

If many are employed in the same duty, all must labor with a perfect conformity of views, feelings, and conduct.

There must be no jealousies or divisions; you must not listen to reports against those with whom you are working; you must avoid haughtiness and quickness of temper; you must not spare yourself; you should, as far as possible, choose for your part what is most difficult; you should not attribute the good result to yourself, and should gladly yield to the views of others in all that is permitted.

You should never, unnecessarily, take a part of the time consecrated to your spiritual exercises, under pretext of discharging your duty.

To excuse the omission of pious exercises, we vainly pretend that we are overwhelmed with work. When we know how to manage our time well, we find enough for everything; but we often lose very much time by giving ourselves up to frivolous occupations and useless conversations, and we afterward fail in essential matters.

Our employment ought to be a means of sanctification; it should never cause us to neglect our pious exercises, which give strength in the perfect discharge of our duties, draw down the blessing of God on our labor, make us attain evenness of temper in the pains and difficulties which we meet with, and, in a word, which give us the means of doing what we have come into religious life for, viz.: the attainment of our salvation.

What a Religious, Employed in Manual Labor, Ought to do, to Render his Work Sweet and Meritorious.

To render your daily occupations agreeable and meritorious: 1. Do not fail to offer your work to God in the morning. 2. Unite yourself to the intentions and dispositions of our Saviour, of whom it is written: "I am poor and in labors from my youth." 3. Love labor, for, as St. Augustine says, nothing is painful to him who loves, and, if he suffer, his pain becomes a joy. 4. Do, with constancy, care, activity, and in the spirit of obedience, penance, and prayer, everything that is commanded you.

The sight of a picture, a look toward heaven, the hour which strikes, will serve as a memorial to you to sanctify your occupations, and will become to you an easy means of keeping yourself in the presence of God, and of inflaming your heart with the most lively love. Do not forget, above all, in your work, what St. Francis de Sales says on the subject of aspirations: "This kind of prayer may, if need be, supply the place of all others, and all others never could supply the place of this. All occupations, all labors, and all spiritual exercises, without these aspirations, are like heaven without stars, and a tree without leaves."

How happy you would be, if you observed these pious practices; instead of being obliged to say, as the apostles said to Jesus Christ: "Master, we have toiled all night and have taken nothing:" for you, there would not be a single action, not a sigh, not a drop of sweat, but would be changed into a precious stone to adorn your eternal crown !

Jesus at Nazareth, the Consolation of a Religious Charged with a Temporal Employment.

A religious, charged with an humble or a difficult temporal employment, in order to appreciate his position, and excite himself to fulfil his duties perfectly, has but to take a look at the hidden life of Jesus at Nazareth. In fact, what does he see? The man-God, the uncreated Wisdom, who possesses, in an infinite degree, all the secrets of knowledge; Jesus, the King of glory, the Lord of lords, in whom are enclosed all the treasures of nature and grace; he, who has come into this world, only to dissipate error, to destroy vice, and to sanctify and save the human race,—the Redeemer, expected for so many ages ! O incomprehensible mystery! He is among men, and men do not suspect it; and, far from drawing them to himself, by enlightening their eyes with some rays of his divine beauty, he seems to withdraw himself from their sight, leading, in the midst of them, not only the most ordinary life, but, to judge by appearances, the most insignificant and most useless one, and one utterly unworthy of himself and his high destiny. He lives in an unknown suburb, in a workshop; he gains his bread by the sweat of his brow, like the poorest of artisans. Yes, this God, who has created the world, who poises it on his fingers; this master of the universe, is engaged in labor, which is the lot of a dependent condition among men! O heaven! was it thus that those days, on which you founded so many hopes, should pass away?

To extinguish in you every ambitious desire, and to make you resigned to your position, however obscure and useless, you need only consider what passed at Nazareth. Who is this child, this youth, this young man, whom the august Trinity is contemplating there, and whom the angels are adoring? Who is this workman? How carefully he avoids notice! How long he remains in his hidden life! O consoling truth! with which you cannot be too much penetrated í During the thirty years of an existence seemingly so ordinary, and even so useless, in the judgment of human wisdom, the life of Jesus Christ was such, that it is impossible to imagine one more perfect, or more useful to the world: his days, in appearance so empty, could not be more full, nor full of more excellent works. Far from his talents being buried, they were employed in a way the most glorious for heaven, and the most profitable for the earth. So that, if, by an impossibility, he had gone forth, from this deep obscurity, before the time which was in the order of the eternal decrees; if, instead of remaining unknown, even to the inhabitants of the village in which he lived, he had made Jerusalem, Rome, and the whole world resound with the sound of his name; if he had been seen to raise the dead or convert the people, not only would he have lived imperfectly, but, while appearing to do great things, he would have done nothing, or what he might have done, would have counted as nothing. Why? Because he would not have done the will of his Father.

Your perfection, your greatness, and your true happiness, do not consist in drawing upon yourself the esteem and affection of creatures, but only in meriting the love of God by the accomplishment of his adorable will. Jesus Christ was as pleasing to his heavenly Father in the exercise of an humble trade at Nazareth, as in his sacrifice on Calvary. In the same way, you can please the Lord in an employment the most obscure and the most despised by men, when it has been assigned to you by Providence, as well as in the most brilliant service. Love, then, the position to which Providence calls you, and desire no other; since the way to be happy, to be holy, and to receive abundant graces, is to do what God wishes of us, and to do it as he wills. Ask for nothing, desire nothing; be content with the situation in which you are. It is not what we do, but the way in which it is done, which makes us truly great. How many are saved in an humble position, who would be lost in more elevated duties! How many religious have procured more glory for God in manual labor than others in more important positions! Abandon yourself entirely to the will of God, and say, with St. Ignatius: "I would rather, O Lord! be a worm of the earth, if thou didst desire it, than be a seraph against thy will."

ON THE DUTY OF TEACHING.

Sublimity of the Duties of a Religious Teacher of Youth.

To educate children, to teach them to know God, to love him, and to serve him; to instruct them in their duties to Jesus Christ, our divine Redeemer, and to Mary, our august Mother; to make them virtuous and instructed members of society, citizens devoted to their country and order, Christians faithful to the Church, and saints for heaven,—in the light of faith, and even of reason, is the greatest, the most elevated, and the most meritorious work which a simple Christian can accomplish upon earth.

"I have examined in vain," said the illustrious Chancellor Gerson, "and I find no more glorious duty than that of educating youth. What a happiness to preserve for the Holy Spirit those sanctuaries in which he delights to dwell! How God loves to be served by these pure souls! With what joy he accepts the first-fruits of their affections, and the offering of a heart which the infected air of the world has not yet contaminated! How important, then, it is to give all my care to preserve, increase, and strengthen in them these good sentiments, and to prevent the perversity of the world from stifling their rising virtues !

" No, I see nothing greater than to snatch these children from the perverseness and contagion with which the enemy of the human race seeks to poison their souls, even at the most tender age. Oh, what a noble undertaking is that of destroying the work of the devil, and of drawing these young souls from the gates of hell; of planting, in the garden of the Church, those little saplings which are the delight of Jesus Christ; of cultivating them, of watering them, and of making them the ornament of the garden of this heavenly spouse ! "

Thus the holy fathers are at a loss with what name to honor this employment. They call it a royal, apostolic, angelic, and divine office.

It is a royal duty, because, says St. Clement of Alexandria, the office of a king is to save the people. It is an apostolic function, because, according to St. Jerome, it is the office of the apostles, whom Jesus Christ has appointed to be the masters, teachers, and saviours of men. It is an angelical office: this is why St. John Chrysostom calls those who fill it, the substitutes of angels, because they perform their office. Lastly, it is a divine office: those who are called to it are not only substitutes for angels, but, in a certain way, they are substitutes for the Divinity, since all the occupation of God is to labor for our salvation. They represent the person of our Saviour, whose office it was to instruct the ignorant, to convert sinners, to preach the gospel to the poor, to draw men away from the power of the devil, and to sacrifice his life for their salvation.

Oh, how happy should every religious devoted to teaching consider himself in being called to this holy duty, and with what care should he study to make himself worthy of it!

To accomplish this noble duty:—

1. He will every day implore the assistance of God, the protection of the Blessed Virgin, of St. Joseph, his glorious patron, and of the holy guardian angels of the children intrusted to his care.

2. He will study, with attention and perseverance, the most efficacious means of securing the success of the education and instruction which he is called to give to his pupils, according to the particular dispositions of their spirit and heart.

What a Christian School Ought to be.

It is in the highest degree important that you should understand well the sublime nature of your functions, and the end which you should propose to yourself in their fulfilment. To do this, meditate frequently on the following beautiful passage, in which is contained all that can be said, which is most elevated, most just, and most striking, on the employment which you have to perform:—

"Christian schools are the seminaries or nurseries of the Church and state, in which children, like young trees, are raised, to be transplanted hereafter into different conditions, and to bring forth fruit in due season; in fact, it is in these places that virtue is cultivated, and the vicious habits of corrupt nature are corrected by the Christian education which is there given them.

"Christian schools are the novitiate of Christianity, in which children are formed in the Christian religion, into which they have entered by baptism, just as religious are formed, in their novitiate, for the religious state in which they are to make profession; and as, usually, there are no good professed in the different religious congregations of the Church except those who have been good novices, so there are no good Christians but those who have been good pupils.

"Christian schools are, 1st: asylums for children against the corruption of the world; 2d, places of safety in which to shelter their innocence, and to preserve the inestimable treasure of baptismal grace; 3d, refuges for those who have already begun to lose their innocence in the midst of the world; 4th, they are public courses, established to teach the science of salvation and the practice of Christian virtues.

"These schools are holy academies where children are prepared for the spiritual warfare which they will have to make or sustain, all their life, against the enemies of their salvation; where they are instructed in the means, and where the necessary weapons are given them, to come out always victorious from this kind of combats.

"It is also there that the children begin to be formed into wise workmen, faithful magistrates, good fathers of families, pious ecclesiastics, and holy religious.

"Christian schools are, as it were, the churches of children, because there they adore God, address their prayers to him, sing his praises, and learn to love and serve him. There they are taught to practise virtue, to avoid vice, and to follow Christian maxims; there, too, they are taught to pray to God, to make their confessions well, and to communicate worthily.

"Take away Christian schools, and you sap the foundation of religion; the field of the Church will not fail to become waste, and bring forth briers and thorns; ignorance, like a thick cloud, will not be long in spreading over the surface of the world, and corruption, like a rushing torrent, will soon overflow and flood the earth which is deprived of this help.

"In fact, what may we not fear and apprehend when the instruction of children ceases, when their education is neglected, when they are no longer corrected, and when they are left to themselves? When they are grown up, they will people the Church with children who will cover her with shame; families, with members who will be their scourge, and, in fine, they will people hell with reprobates."*

How sublime and important are your functions! Oblige yourselves, therefore, to discharge them worthily.

---

*This beautiful passage is found in the Life of the Ven. J. B. de La Salle, by Canon Bellin.

What a Christian Teacher should Propose to Himself.

What is a Christian teacher, charged with the education of young people? He is a man into whose hands Jesus Christ has confided a certain number of children, whom he has purchased with his blood, and for whom he has given his life; in whom he dwells as in his house or temple; whom he looks upon as his members, his brethren, and his coheirs, who will reign with him, and will glorify God through him for all eternity. And for what end has he intrusted them to him? To preserve in them the precious and inestimable character of innocence which he has imprinted on their souls in baptism, to make them true Christians.

This, then, is the end and object of the education of children: everything else is but a means. Whence it follows that a master ought to have very great care to form them for religion. Thus, he will apply himself to instruct them in the mysteries of faith, especially in all points necessary to make their faith explicit; he will instruct them in the Creed, in the truths relating to Christian life, such as the commandments of God and of the Church, and the requisite dispositions for receiving the sacraments with fruit, etc.

He will not fail to speak to them of the obligations of baptism, of the renunciations which they have made in receiving that sacrament, of the esteem which they ought to have for it, of the graces which they have received in it, and of what they are obliged to do to preserve them.

He will explain to them all that relates to the obligations of assisting at the divine service, of hearing holy Mass on Sundays and holydays of obligation, of the precious fruits which they will gather from doing so every day, of the manner of fulfilling this important duty, and of behavior in church, as well as regards the interior as the exterior.

He will teach them the necessity of prayer, how and at what time this essential duty should be discharged, as in the morning, at night, and in an infinity of other circumstances of life. He will require them to know the ordinary formulas to be used in prayer, and to pronounce them distinctly and well, when they recite them.

He will teach them how to make their actions meritorious, by offering them to God, and by beseeching his help to do them well; besides, how they ought to profit by trials and afflictions; how they should submit with resignation to the will of God, in sickness and in the other trying events of this life; how they should fulfil the duties of their state, avoid the occasions of sin, and never be the cause of scandal to others, etc.

He will make them understand well the Christian and moral virtues: faith, hope, charity, justice, goodness, uprightness of heart, wisdom, prudence, fortitude, temperance, modesty in discourse and conduct, the respect and submission which they owe to the ecclesiastical and civil powers, the immortality of the soul, the last end of man, grace, sin, etc.

He will inspire them, not only with solid piety toward God and our Lord Jesus Christ, but also with a special devotion to the Most Blessed Virgin, to St. Joseph, to their holy patrons and guardian angels; by teaching them the reason for these devotions, and by rewarding those who most delight in them. He will add, on suitable occasions, striking traits from the lives of the saints and of illustrious men.

Lastly, he will inculcate incessantly on them the obligation they are under of preferring their salvation to everything else; and, by all these instructions, he will form in them the qualities which make a good Christian, a good citizen, a good soldier, a good merchant, etc., according to the different states to which each will be called by Divine Providence.*

Reward of Religious Devoted to Teaching.

"O the beautiful and rich crowns," says Fr. Crasset, "which God prepares for a religious who inspires little children with a horror of vice and a love of virtue! Those, says the Holy Spirit, 'who instruct others unto justice, shall shine like stars for all eternity,' because they are enlightened in time with the light of their teaching and good example.

"There are different mansions in heaven; there are thrones of glory differing from one another; all are not equal in grandeur, but the Son of God assures us that the highest are for those who have done good, and have taught it. And where will a religious be placed who instructs youth, with very great labor and pains, who teaches them to gain temporal and eternal life, and who does this gratuitously, without expecting any reward,

---

*These passages are taken from "Twelve Virtues of a Good Master," a valuable work, the diligent perusal of which we cannot too highly recommend.

from a pure and disinterested charity, and by the voluntary renunciation of his liberty, in order to devote himself to a state of life so poor and so laborious, so useful for heaven and earth, so necessary for the Church, so useful to the public good, so pleasing to God, and so profitable to every one?

"What a comforting assurance will he have at his death, after having spent his life in this exercise of patience and charity! 'He who causeth a sinner to be converted from the error of his way, shall save his soul from death, and shall cover a multitude of sins.' Oh! what, then, can the religious fear, who has drawn a multitude of souls from hell, who has sanctified a large number of families, who has prevented an infinity of crimes, who has planted and rooted in hearts an infinity of virtues; who praises God with as many mouths as he has taught children to pray; who serves him with as many hands as he has prepared for labor and the practice of virtue; who loves him with as many hearts as he has inflamed with the fire of charity; who has made him known to little infidels, adored by little atheists, loved by little savages, and who has given him an infinity of sceptres, crowns, and empires, since the heart of man is the kingdom of God?

"If the Lord promises to reward, on the day of judgment, him who has given to a poor man a cup of water in his name, what crown does he not prepare for him who abandons his goods and sacrifices his liberty, in order to communicate the treasures of wisdom to poor children? And if he will thank those who shall have given to the least of men the goods of the body, which he calls the "treasure of iniquity," what will not be his obligation to those who dispense to little children, whom he cherishes so tenderly, and who are in the utmost poverty, the goods of the spirit and the treasures of grace?

"Oh, what consolation will a good religious have, at the hour of death, when he sees all the souls which he has sent on to heaven, come to his assistance! The guardian angels of all the children whom he has instructed will come to console him; all the souls which he has sanctified will form a beautiful crown around his bed, and will bear his soul into the bosom of Abraham, amid canticles of glory and rejoicing.

"Oh, how great is the merit of your profession, since you procure the greatest of all goods for the noblest and yet most indigent of creatures, from a pure and disinterested motive of charity, and with incredible labors!"

The Love which a Young Teacher should Have for his Duties, and the Zeal with which he should Discharge them.

After the considerations which have gone before, we shall not have need to insist much, in order to make you understand the love which you ought to have for your office. In fact, how can you not love such sublime functions, while you have in your heart a little love for Jesus Christ, and zeal for the salvation of souls?

Yes, love the office which is so useful to the children and to the Church, and which is so fitted to procure the glory of God and your own sanctification.

Love your duties; for, on the greater or less love with which you discharge them, will depend the good of a number of children, and, I will also say, almost your own salvation.

Love your duties; for, generally, we only do well what we do from love; and here the question relates to one of the noblest works of the apostolate intrusted to the Church, our mother.

Not only ought you to love your duties, but it is an essential obligation for you to devote yourself entirely to them, so as to discharge them well.

Cowardice and negligence are not permitted on so important a point. Not to use all your endeavors to bring up your pupils in a Christian way, would be to render yourself guilty before God, religion, society, the children, the community, and yourself.

It is not the same with education as it is in other careers. If you were a laborer, an artisan, or a soldier, and you had not the necessary qualities for your calling, it would be a misfortune, doubtless, but you alone would suffer by it; while, in the service of education, you could not be either bad or indifferent without compromising the future, here and hereafter, of your pupils. The evil caused by your negligence will be immense; and the children will have to regret eternally their precious years, or, which is still worse, they will have received such bad impressions, that it will be impossible ever to efface them.

See, then, how awful your duties are before God and men, and understand how much devotedness they require on your part.

If you do not acquit yourself of them with zeal and ardor—

You will be ungrateful and perjured before our Lord, who has intrusted to you the object of the predilections of his heart.

You will be disobedient to your superiors, in a matter of the highest importance.

You will fail in one of your most essential duties.

You will do an irreparable wrong to the youth confided to your care.

You will assume a terrible responsibility on your own head.

If there should be only one child who is a victim of your neglect; if there should be only one, who, through your fault, should, later on, lead a bad life, how great would be the evil! A child of God, his well-beloved, through your fault, would become his enemy and the child of Satan! Innocence, the price of the blood of Jesus Christ, would be lost! The glorious image of God would be debased! The living temple of the Holy Ghost would be profaned and filled with the abominations of sin! And more than this, how many souls cannot one wicked soul drag with it into the abyss! One single infected sheep is enough to spread contagion in the whole flock.

Now, would not all these evils, the consequence of the misconduct of that child, be imputed to your guilty neglect?

Love, then, your duties, and devote yourself, body and soul, to fulfil them with all the zeal and perfection of which you are capable.

How Useful Piety is to a Teacher.

"Of all qualities," said the virtuous Rollin, "the most necessary for a master is piety." Knowledge, devotedness, and the most brilliant qualities, cannot supply its place. Do you wish to be truly a worthy teacher of youth, oblige yourself to acquire that solid piety which makes you refer everything to God, and which has him alone for its end; that, in the great work of education, you only seek the salvation of souls and the glory of God. "Christian teachers," says Fr. Judde, "ought to excite in their souls an infinite esteem of perfection, to burn with an ardent desire of pleasing God, and to act, as far as possible, in imitation of our Lord. If a person languishes in the pursuit of perfection, he will necessarily fail in his duties toward his scholars; for the care of young people is essentially the fruit of our extreme ardor for virtue, and, as it were, an outpouring of the superabundance of the Holy Spirit, who lives in us. The experience of all ages proves with what cowardice and with what a servile spirit he is filled who, engaged in education, does not work for God, and is satisfied with obeying while he is under the eye of the superior. If at times he fulfils exactly his duties as a teacher, this does not arise from a desire of doing good, but only from a human motive, as, for example, the satisfaction of self-love or the fear of reproach. Deprived of the interior strength which zeal brings with it, he will be inconstant in doing his duty, and will fail in the performance of it, as often as the fear of men is not urging him on."

Reason confirms the language of experience. In fact, how will a master form his pupils in virtue, if he does not labor to acquire it himself?

Without virtue, he will not have that constant and untiring application, that patience and continual gentleness; or, in a word, that charity, which is so necessary in his position.

Without virtue, he will not sufficiently understand the principles of the spiritual life to be able to explain them, and cause them to be followed.

Without virtue, he will not possess the art of cultivating in hearts that seed which is not in his own; for, that which goes to the heart must come from it.

Without virtue, in a word, he will not be able to serve as a guide to his pupils in the way that St. Paul requires, when he says: "Be imitators of me, as I am also of Christ." And, indeed, without good example, what can he do?

ON THE DUTY OF TEACHING.

If, then, you wish to discharge your duties with pleasure, fruit, and merit, cherish in yourself the spirit of piety, by the faithful discharge of your religious duties.

Obligation of a Teacher to Give Good Example to his Pupils.

Does the salvation of your pupils or your own salvation move you? Take to heart, and imprint in the depth of your soul, this essential rule: "To give always a good example, and never to be, in your conduct, either light or indifferent."

You cannot use too much circumspection in presence of your pupils. All have their eyes fixed on you, and they are quicker to discern than we might be led to believe. Sometimes they notice a fault, to which you have paid no attention; and this fault shocks them, and makes you more contemptible in their eyes than a more serious fault would have done in those of grown people. A single moment of forgetfulness, during which you have let them perceive the weak side of your soul, is enough to efface the good impression of your teaching, and to pave the way for another fault more dangerous.

Children have their judgment too slightly

developed, to distinguish a small fault from one which is more important, a human weakness from a bad and premeditated one. We cannot be too watchful in the presence of such judges. It would be to show a very small knowledge of the mind of children, not to believe in the necessity of guarding yourself, and practising an extreme reserve in their presence. You will nowhere find so little indulgence.

Do not, then, neglect any means or any occasion of teaching virtue by your words and example. Every Christian should be an example to his neighbor: with how much greater reason should the teacher be so to his pupils? If, then, you have any love for yourself, if you have a little affection for your pupils; if you love the Lord, above all things, take care to give a good example of good works. Enlighten your pupils with your knowledge, and show them, by your conduct, what a true servant of God is, in spirit and in truth, so that, seeing your good works, following your example, they may give glory to God, and edify their neighbor. What good might not a religious do whose pupils say: Our teacher is a Saint!

"Recall to mind, frequently," says Fr. Judde, "that children learn more by the eyes than by the ears. Let them see you very recollected in church, and never by your manner leave any doubt in their minds whether you are praying or not. Make them have respect for the things of God, by the respectful manner in which you always speak of him; inspire them with gentleness by your patience and equanimity; with modesty, by your modesty and demeanor; with affability, by your mode of life and honorable manner, and with horror of sin by your irreproachable conduct. You will never attain to all this, if you are not really such as you seem to be. You cannot long make pretence; a moment of natural excitement will quickly make evident what you have for a long time tried to dissemble. You ought to be the visible angel of your pupils: what a terrible thing, if you become their devil! Oh! far better, with a millstone about your neck, to have been cast into the sea, than to have scandalized one of these little ones so dear to God!

Obligation of a Teacher to Apply to Study.

It is no longer the age when you can hope to promote the greater glory of God without the aid of human knowledge. The wisest, it is true, are not always the greatest apostles, but it is certain that a learned man, if he is holy, has the advantage over one who is holy, but not learned. Since you ought to desire to use all possible means to procure the glory of God, his spirit will lead you most surely to instruct yourself in a solid manner.

To labor to advance in human science is, moreover, one of the most efficacious means of filling our schools with numerous pupils. Many fathers of family, careless, alas! in religious matters, would not send us their children, if we promised only to educate them in a Christian manner: they only consent to let us make good Christians of their children, on the one condition that they shall receive in our classes an education superior, or at least equal, to that which they would receive elsewhere.

Besides, to neglect study is not to do what you are obliged to do, and it is, too often, doing many things which you ought not to do. Fr. Judde, speaking to young religious, said: "I do not look upon study for you simply as one of those duties of zeal and charity so essential to our state of life, but as a duty of the strictest justice. Religion is obliged to form us with great care and pains, to take care of us in health and sickness, and charitably to provide for our real wants, whatever they may be. But, on our part, we are also obliged to second her care, in order to become useful instruments for the different duties she imposes on us; to serve her, and to discharge her various obligations to the public and our benefactors, and, for this end, neither to spare our natural talents, our industry, our strength, our health, nor even our life, if this is necessary.

"If a hired servant is justly taxed with injustice when he receives the price of his day's labor, after having lost several hours of it, are you not equally responsible for the loss of your time?

"And if, later, a lawful service is demanded from you, and you cannot render it through your lack of preparedness, would you feel quiet in your conscience?

"But let us pass by these reasons, which are too weak for a well-intentioned friend of God, and let us say that, if the obligation of work did not exist for you, you ought, just the same, to impose it upon yourself, in order to avoid the many faults which loss of time brings with it.

"An idle man is not alone one who absolutely does nothing; a man who does only trifling things, or who does anything else but what he ought to do, or who permits what is evil by his carelessness, is also called by this name. If you do not impose upon yourself serious work during your free time, you will be much exposed to the danger of falling into one of these faults. How, in fact, will you employ your free time, without a fixed plan of studies? You will occupy yourself in profane or frivolous reading. You will go to tell or ask for news, perhaps murmur against your superiors, blame your equals, and speak evil of your inferiors. What an account to render to Almighty God at the end of your day! And, when the year has rolled by in this way, and when this state of things has lasted for many years, what a terrible responsibility, if, by negligence and idleness, you are incapable of discharging your duty well!"

Make, therefore, a serious resolution to labor usefully for your own instruction. Make it a conscientious obligation.

Employ your free moments so much the more carefully, as they are less frequent. Of all the acts of virtue which you can make, application to study in the spirit of faith and zeal is one of the most pleasing to God.

Dangers against which a Young Teacher Should Arm himself.

On leaving the novitiate, you will find yourself thrown into the midst of a life of activity and excitement, into the midst of a little noisy and tumultuous crowd, and this kind of life has its dangers. A good religious ought to expect not to have a moment's rest or a moment of free time. The mind being always full of his pupils, of their needs, studies, the little contrarieties which he experiences, and the means of success to be tried, he will hardly be occupied with his own interests. There results from this an interior dissipation, which, if it be not carefully watched, is injurious to the pious calm and to that life of solitude and recollection, which is so much recommended to you. Another danger is that of being too much attached to the children: not that you can ever lavish too much care on them, but that, having renounced everything for God, you might form new bonds, and cherish an affection which is too human.

When you see, among the children, upright, frank, and candid souls who are led to what is good and to piety with a sweet attraction, the success of whom crowns your efforts; who, with their attractive ways, know how to gain the affection, and repay with gratitude the kindness, of their teachers, it is difficult to prevent an involuntary impression of interest and attachment, and not to experience for these good children a paternal affection, which one distrusts so much the less, as it is hidden under a pretext of zeal and duty, and of which one does not perceive the sad consequences, until it is too late to prevent them. Moreover, the danger of these feelings, carried too far, would excite that interest which religion should moderate; it would lead us to identify ourselves with these children, so as to forget ourselves for them, to be entirely occupied, or rather preoccupied, with them, so that the remembrance of them should follow us everywhere, disturb us in our prayer, and leave us no freedom of mind. It would perhaps create in our hearts those too lively affections which encourage a dangerous straining of the mind, furnish weapons to the enemy of our salvation; and as a spark is able to kindle a conflagration, it would also overwhelm our soul at the time of separation, which in the nature of circumstances must come upon us, and would form too close ties, which these young people would encourage by visits and too familiar conversations. There is

ON THE DUTY OF TEACHING. 185

also to be feared the danger of independence; that is to say, that, left to ourselves in the midst of the class, obliged to make ourselves respected and to give orders, this passing from obedience to command, or the return from command to obedience, is apt to expose us to the great danger of making that passive docility more difficult, as also that submission of the will, which we can indeed curb and restrain, but which always tries to react and rise up again. These are the principal dangers. We point them out to you, so that, being on your guard, it may be easy for you to avoid them.

General Means Suitable for Securing the Success of a Religious whose Life is devoted to Teaching.

To succeed in his sublime mission, a religious, whose life is devoted to teaching, ought to inspire in his pupils the following sentiments: he must make himself esteemed, loved, respected, and feared.

1. A teacher succeeds in making himself *esteemed* by his pupils, when he shows wisdom in his conduct, and capacity in his teaching: thus, 1, he ought never to say or do anything which would not be found just and proper

by every person of good sense and reason ; 2, he ought not to venture to give a lesson, without knowing it perfectly : whence arises the necessity of well preparing all, but especially religious instructions, the catechism, and the reflections for each day. Experience shows that, when a teacher gives evidence of his capacity in his religious teaching, he acquires the esteem, and, often, the affection of his pupils, even of those who are less disposed in his favor.

2. A teacher is sure of making himself *beloved* by his pupils, when, having been able to gain their esteem, he joins, to a great equanimity of conduct, a great amiability of character, and when, in his manner of action, as well as in his words, he manifests devotedness and benevolence.

Another very powerful means of acquiring their affection is to teach them every day something which they did not know before, and to encourage them, at the proper time, with some kind words and an air of approval, which show them that you are pleased with their efforts and success.

3. If a teacher, esteemed and beloved by his pupils, knows how to respect himself at all times, and to keep his position and dignity, he will necessarily make himself respected.

But, whatever may be the esteem and affection of pupils for their teacher, he should never forget that familiarity breeds contempt, and that, whatever may be the satisfaction which he has to manifest, there should always be an invincible barrier between them and himself.

4. Esteem, love, and respect of the pupils for the teacher are not always sufficient to keep them to their duty : hence the necessity for the teacher to make himself *feared*, and to inspire them with the fear of losing his esteem and his favor, and even of incurring some punishment. But, if he is prudent and wise, he will only make use of this means with the utmost discretion, so guiding their sensibility, as to preserve the moral influence which he may have acquired over their minds and hearts.

For the rest, he will take great care to prevent the faults of his pupils, and will be able often to pardon them, when there does not appear any ill-will or obstinate idleness.

Principal Means of Keeping Order in Class.

A teacher should neglect nothing to procure order, without which there can never be any progress, piety, or morality in the class. For this, he must make use of the following means, with fidelity and perseverance:—

1. *Silence.*—A young teacher should be extremely chary of his words: the less he speaks, the less he is fatigued, and the more his pupils listen to him and are silent.

2. *Vigilance.*—To see all that happens in the class-room, so that the pupils may know that they cannot fail in their duty without being noticed. To remain at your seat as much as possible is the *surveillance* which is best. How many faults cannot a watchful teacher prevent! What disorders, on the other hand, are not brought on by negligence! Every young teacher ought to look upon this as a very important point.

3. Keep your pupils constantly employed. As soon as you perceive that any one is not working, make him a sign to go over his lesson again.

4. As soon as one exercise is finished, begin the next, without giving the children time to be distracted.

5. Avoid everything which might cause noise, disorder, and dissipation.

6. When you hear a noise, you can stop every lesson by a stroke of the bell; give some privilege to the one who seems to be most attentive, and impose a penance on the most troublesome.

7. Use all necessary precautions for keep-

ing silence during moving or changing of place, etc.

8. Avoid putting two children on penance, near each other.

9.. Impose a task on every child who is on penance,.if it be only to learn a line or two by heart.

10. Avoid all fretful, angry, or impatient ways, and all facial contortions calculated to provoke ridicule.

11. Choose the monitors with the greatest care.

12. Ask for advice, and never engage, of your own accord, in a doubtful course.

13. Be always so consistent in your conduct, that the pupils may be convinced that what you approve to-day you will approve to-morrow and every day, and you will be able to enforce what you require.

14. On your return from class, examine yourself seriously as to the manner in which it has been conducted, on the means you have made use of to secure good order and progress.

Important Advice.

1. Never use the children roughly, nor shake nor strike them in any possible way.

2. If a pupil should be unusually troublesome and disobedient, if he refuse to do his penance, you can put him in a corner until the next visit of the director.

3. Never be familiar with any child, never touch or caress him, or speak to him in private; do not place him near you, do not make him remain in the class after the others, nor permit him to go with you to any part of the house.

4. Never allow yourself to pull the children about, under pretence of changing their place, or of making them go forward or backward; nor take toys out of their pockets, etc.

5. Be perfectly convinced that the children will never fail to tell their parents all that a teacher says or does in class: and, consequently, never allow yourself an action, step or word, which might compromise you.

6. Study to give good example at all times.

Conduct, when you do not Succeed in Class.

It happens sometimes that young teachers, seeing their efforts fail, are very much tempted to be discouraged. Take care of acting thus; wait for such time as God may see fit to aid us, and only anticipate it by your holy desires and fervent prayers. Do not forget

ON THE DUTY OF TEACHING. 191

that nothing is more beautiful, greater, or more adorable than the will of God, and that your zeal ought to consist in doing his good pleasure. If the Lord subjects you to this painful, though meritorious, trial, as a rule follow these counsels:—

1. Do not be cast down at the first obstacles: we do not become good teachers in a single day. How many are there who, after having met with serious difficulties at the beginning, have become excellent teachers afterward!

2. Examine the causes of your want of success, and apply the best remedy you can.

3. Humbly make known your difficulties, and faithfully follow the advice you receive.

4. Do all that you possibly can, and be resigned.

5. Above all things put your trust in God, offer him your difficulties, and expect everything from him.

6. Remember that you are not obliged to succeed, but to do all that you can: God rewards labor, and not success.

7. Often beg, in your prayers and communions, the grace which is necessary to discharge your duty well.

8. Take sometimes, as the subject of your meditation, the consoling thoughts given farther on.

God is not slow in blessing those who are animated with these sentiments: they end by fulfilling their duties, not only with success, but often with distinction.

If, because you do not succeed in a class, superiors think fit to remove you from it, resign yourself willingly, and discharge your new duty with all the fidelity which you are capable of, without allowing yourself to give way to grief, disquiet, disgust, or to an ill-founded fear of not doing sufficiently well. The only good which God demands from us, is that which is commanded by obedience.

Consoling Thoughts, which a Teacher, who does not Succeed in his Office, should Meditate upon.

You find that it is difficult to govern children, to bear with their defects, and to be the object of their ingratitude: did it cost Jesus Christ nothing to redeem mankind, to expiate your sins, and to merit heaven for you? Was our Divine Master discouraged at the sight of humiliations and sufferings? Behold the sadness of Jesus in the Garden of Olives, his humiliations and sufferings in the prætorium and on Calvary! See his sweat of blood, his flesh torn in pieces, his head crowned with thorns, and his body nailed to the cross! After that, can you say: "My employment is too difficult, too painful; it exposes me to calumny, persecution, and ingratitude; it costs too much to do good to children"?

For love of you, Jesus Christ has suffered all. For love of him, can you bear nothing? Where are your faith, courage and gratitude?

"He who loves, embraces with pleasure the most painful and bitter things for the sake of his beloved, and does not turn away from whatever trying circumstances may arise."

"Love makes light everything which is heavy, and supports with equanimity all the inequalities of life; for it carries the burden, without feeling its weight, and makes what is bitter, sweet and light." ("Imitation.")

Oh! if you loved Jesus Christ, how happy would you think yourself to have something to suffer for his glory! Far from complaining, you would say with St. Francis Xavier: "Still more, O Lord, still more!"

"If you partake of the sufferings of Christ, rejoice." (1 Pet. iv, 13.)

"Labor as a good soldier of Christ Jesus." (2 Tim. ii, 3.)

"He who surmounts courageously the difficulties of his office, is the conqueror of himself, the master of the world, the friend of Jesus Christ, and the heir of heaven!" ("Imitation.")

"As our Lord Jesus Christ," says Fr. Lallemant, "has redeemed the world only by his cross, death, and the shedding of his blood, and not by his miracles or preaching, so the laborers of the gospel apply the graces of redemption only by their crosses, and by the persecutions which they suffer. So that they ought not to expect the reward of their labors, if they are not accompanied by crosses and sufferings.

"We must not consider our afflictions as evils which cause us to suffer, nor as mortifications which lower us in the eyes of the world: we should look upon them, according to the example of our Lord, in the eternal designs of God, in the order of his providence, and in the view of his love toward us; in the heart of Jesus Christ, who has chosen them for us, and who presents them to us as the material for the crowns which he is preparing for us, and as a trial of our virtue and fidelity in his service."

To sustain you in the difficulties of your employment, often call to mind :—

1. *The sins which you have committed.*—In expiation of your faults, God will accept willingly the troubles which you meet with in

ON THE DUTY OF TEACHING. 195

your employment. Can you find them too great,—you who have deserved hell?

2. *The example of the saints.*—What have they not done for Jesus Christ? With what courage, resignation, and happiness have they not borne trials a thousand times more severe than yours! What are your troubles and your labors compared to those of the apostles, martyrs, missionaries?

3. *The fruit of your labors.*—If you discharge your duty in a holy manner, what good will you not accomplish! What sins you will avoid! How many virtues you will have practised! To the salvation of how many souls you will contribute! Your duty is laborious; but it is profitable to your pupils, to their families, to society and to the Church! Oh, how pleasant it is to God and profitable to yourself!

4. *The reward which is promised to you.*—How beautiful and rich will be the crown which God is preparing for the religious who inspires children with a horror of sin and a love of virtue! "They, that instruct many unto justice shall shine like stars for all eternity." (Dan. xii, 3.)

"If the labor frightens you, let the reward encourage you." (St. Bernard.)

Oh, if, like Stephen, you should see the

heavens opened, and Jesus Christ holding in his hand the crown which he is preparing for you, you would complain, not of suffering, but of not suffering more ! Far from asking for consolation and repose, you would say with the heroic Theresa: "Lord ! to suffer or die, to suffer or die !" Look at your crosses in the wounds of Jesus Christ. Mingle your bitterness with that of his chalice.

Think that your divine Saviour has a share in all your troubles, and bears them in a certain sense with you. Yes, do not doubt, he is unceasingly with you; he sees all that you do and all that you bear for him.

In your troubles, have recourse to prayer: he who permits the trial for your good, will give you the strength to bear it.

Call Mary to your aid, and she will obtain strength and consolation for you.

Invoke the saints who have sanctified themselves in the performance of the same duties as yourself.

In trying moments, say from the bottom of your heart: "My God, I accept all that thou willest in the way that thou willest, and as much as thou willest."*

---

* See Vercruysse's Meditations, vol. ii, page 344.

OF CATECHISM.

Excellence of the Catechism.

"THE office of catechist is so important," says the Ven. J. B. de la Salle, "that the holy bishops of the primitive Church looked upon it as their chief duty, and considered it an honor, to instruct the catechumens and new Christians, by explaining the catechism to them. St. Cyril, Patriarch of Jerusalem, and St. Augustine, Bishop of Hippo, have left in writing the catechetical instructions which they gave themselves, and which they had given by priests who assisted them in their pastoral duties; St. Jerome, whose learning was so profound, testifies, in his letter to Leta, that he gained more honor by catechising a young child than by being the teacher of a great monarch. Gerson, High Chancellor of the University of Paris, had so great an esteem of this duty that he exercised it himself during the latter years of his life.

"The reason why these great men esteemed catechetical instruction so much is, that this was the first duty which Jesus Christ intrusted to his apostles. St. Luke relates that, as soon as our Lord had chosen the apostles, he sent them to preach the kingdom of God; it is also this which he commended to them in the most express terms, just before he ascended into heaven, when he said to them: 'Go, therefore, teach all nations; baptizing them in the name of the Father, and of the Son, and of the Holy Ghost.' (Matt. xxviii, 19.) It was the first thing St. Peter did in the temple at Jerusalem, after the descent of the Holy Ghost; and the fruit of this first catechism was the conversion of three thousand persons, who embraced the faith of Jesus Christ; it was also the principal employment of St. Paul, as is evident from his discourse in the Areopagus, and from those discourses delivered before Felix and Festus: he declares the pain which he would feel in going to his disciples, without being useful to them, by instructing and catechising them. Add to this that Jesus Christ was not satisfied with intrusting to his apostles the office of giving catechism; he did the same himself, and taught the principal truths of our religion, as it is related in a number of passages in the Holy Gospels. He said expressly: 'I must preach the kingdom of God; for therefore am I sent.' (Luke iv, 43.)

"Apply these words to yourself, and consider that it is also for this that Jesus Christ has sent you, and that the Church has received you as an auxiliary to her ministers. Make use, then, of all the application which is necessary for this duty, and strive to fulfil it with as much zeal and success as the saints who have discharged it the best.

"We must not be astonished that the bishops of the early Church and the holy apostles should have had so great an esteem of the office of instructing catechumens and new Christians, and that St. Paul, in particular, should have gloried in having been sent to preach the gospel, 'not in wisdom of speech, lest the cross of Christ should be made void' (1 Cor. i, 17), but in simple language, intelligible to the most limited minds. He had drawn these sentiments from the very school of our divine Saviour. The same apostle, penetrated with the excellence of his sublime vocation, cried out that he had received 'the grace to preach among the gentiles the unsearchable riches of Christ.' (Eph. iii, 8.) The fruit of these instructions of this holy apostle was so great, that those who, before hearing them, 'were without

Christ, strangers to the testaments, and having no hope of the promise' (Eph. ii, 12), having embraced the faith, and having, by baptism, been clothed in Jesus Christ, were 'no longer strangers and foreigners; but fellow-citizens with the saints, and domestics with God, and forming part of the edifice which was built upon the foundations of the apostles and prophets' (Eph. ii, 19, 20), and raised by Jesus Christ as a sanctuary, in which God dwells by his Holy Spirit.

"If you consider attentively these wonderful effects of the zeal of the apostles and holy bishops who have succeeded them, you will understand how great is the office of a catechist in the eye of faith; you will animate yourself with a zeal like theirs for this important duty, and you will have a special esteem for the instruction and Christian education of your pupils; because this is the surest means to make them become true children of God and citizens of heaven, and, in a word, because it is the foundation and support of piety, and of all the other good which is in the Church.

"Thank God for a favor which thus associates you with the ministry of the apostles and chief bishops and pastors of the Church, and honor this ministry yourself, by making yourself a worthy minister of the New Testament."

What it is to Give Catechism.

"'To give catechism,' says Mgr. Dupanloup, 'is not only to teach children Christianity, it is to educate them in Christianity.'

"To bring them up in Christianity! Noble word! What does it mean? It is to bring them up in innocence and Christian wisdom, in the light and grace of the evangelical virtues; it is to educate them in the fear and love of God, to prepare them for eternal life, by sanctifying the present one.

"Is it not evident, in truth, that to limit yourself to instructing the children in the elements of Christian doctrine, without giving yourself the trouble of making them love and practise it, without forming in them Christian habits, inclinations or morals, is to do almost nothing for the attainment of the great end, almost nothing for virtue and happiness in this life, and absolutely nothing for the gaining of eternal life?

"What is required here, before all things, and after all things, is to gain their souls to God, as the Prince of the Apostles said. Nobody gainsays this; but, for all this, the important and indispensable thing is to form and educate their wills, as well as their understandings, in the order of divine things, by laying in the depth of the heart, with the light of faith, the love of God and the hopes of eternal life. Without doubt, we may worthily educate the minds of children by teaching the Christian doctrine; but, if we do not wish to mutilate wretchedly the work which we are doing, we must, at the same time, educate the heart by the love of that heavenly doctrine, and of the virtues which it inspires. To enlighten them on their duty is of capital importance, I acknowledge: but of what service will this light be, if it does not make them also love their duties, and feel the happiness of practising them? For this end, to the teaching which you give them, which instructs, you must add reflections which move them, examples which persuade, practices which please, and pious exercises which improve. It is necessary to smooth their character, correct their faults, enlighten and rectify their consciences, and ennoble their sentiments; in fine, it is necessary to elevate their whole soul even to God."

To give catechism, that is, to do the work of the catechist, is evidently much more than to explain it: it is to teach it, to love it;

it is to make it pass from theoretical teaching into real life, as far as possible, at that so tender age on which all the other ages of life depend; it is to form the man, and to establish him solidly in Christian morals and habits.

Thus, we may say, there are three degrees in the work of catechism: there is the catechism recited, the catechism explained, and the catechism practised. The recital without explanation is nothing: what would you think of a catechist who should be satisfied with hearing the catechism, and never explaining it? But the recital and explanation without the practice is scarcely anything; for it is the practice of the catechism alone which makes Christians, forms Christian minds and hearts, and gains for their Creator those souls which Jesus Christ has redeemed with his blood.

Under what Conditions we can Give Catechism well.

"The catechist," says Mgr. Dupanloup again, "is not simply a professor of religion and morals who instructs his scholars more or less; he is a pastor and a father. Those who are intrusted to him are not ordinary scholars, they are children of God, children of the Church, and the sheep of the divine Pastor, redeemed by his cross."

These beautiful and striking expressions of apostolic zeal lead me to say to you the chief thing, without which nothing that I have said so far can be practised, or even understood, and this alone is the grand secret of the work which I wish to lay before you; it is this: The catechist must be a pastor and a father.

For a catechist to be a pastor and a father, there is, as for all paternity, one indispensable condition, viz., love. Yes, love,—the great love of God and of souls. The catechist, above all things, must love the children, and God in the children; he must himself be loved by them, and must make them love God; he must teach them to pray and adore their Creator, to repent of their sins which offend him, and to correct the faults which disfigure their souls.

Inasmuch as you have not taught them to love their Father who is in heaven; inasmuch as you have not taught them to love the Church, which is the mother of the faithful, and that holy house which is called the church, and is the house of God; inasmuch as you have not taught them to love the

Blessed Virgin and heaven, and, I add, to love yourself,—yes, yourself; for it is necessary for them to love you,—you will never succeed in anything with them; inasmuch as you have not made them feel that you love them yourself, that you are their pastor and father, you have not done the work which you have to do here.

Yes, when you have taught and explained to these poor children, with the knowledge and clearness of the most skilful professor, every word of the catechism, if they do not love you, if they do not love God, if they do not love the Blessed Virgin and the saints and angels, yourself, all that is religion in their eyes; if, the day after you have finished teaching the catechism,' they flee from you,— once more, your work is not done; you have explained the catechism and given instructions in vain, you have not even instructed them: for, understand well, they will never have solid instruction of the mind, if they have not received the education of the soul. When you try to instruct them, without, at the same time, elevating their hearts, they are only listening to dried-up, arid, and lifeless instruction.

No, if you have not been able to find out the secret of penetrating to their hearts; if you have never felt yourself, if you do not know how to excite in others, those quiverings of the soul which love and zeal for God produce in men and children, that which secures the divine fruit of Christian teaching will have failed for both yourself and them.

And what I say here—remark it well!—holds good in nature and grace. Yes, the shepherd must love his flock, the catechist must love his children, and the children their catechist; otherwise, he will not be able to educate them, nor even to instruct them as he ought.

The instruction will always be without any charm, if he who gives it does not love those who receive it, and if they who receive it do not love him who gives it. This, then, is the great secret of making the catechism really the education of souls: there is no other. Catechists must love God in their children, and must make them see it. Then the children will love their catechists, and God in their catechists, and wonders will be worked in these young souls.

The Study of Catechism.

What more important than the study of that religion which it is your mission to teach! What knowledge more consoling than that of the beauties and perfections of your God, of the mercies of your Father, and of the greatness of your eternal destiny! What study can open to the mind larger horizons, can be more adapted to strengthen you in the practice of virtue, and in the accomplishment of your duties, than that of the holy law of our Saviour,—of that law, the observance of which constitutes your happiness now, and secures for you in eternity the crown of glory which fadeth not away?

A solid Christian instruction is the necessary foundation of all enlightened piety, and of all perseverance in good. It is a fact of experience that nothing is more fitted to strengthen the religious vocation, and to prevent dangerous falls, than a profound knowledge of religion.

Study, therefore, the catechism to strengthen yourself in the practice of what is good, and to lay the foundation of the edifice of your vocation on the immovable rock of an enlightened and profound conviction; study it, too, on account of the sublime duties which you have to fulfil. You are a teacher of the Christian doctrine: the community has been established for this purpose: you would not be worthy of your name, you would not fulfil the hopes of the Church, if the study of religion and the teaching of the catechism did not hold the first place in your affections, and if they were not the essential object of your endeavors.

Nourish yourself, then, with this divine science, in order to be able to make a healthy and abundant distribution of it to all those who shall be intrusted to your care. If the time which the rule devotes to this study is not fully employed, and if you bring a guilty neglect to this important exercise, you will be like a mother with a barren breast, whose impoverished milk cannot support her child, nor prevent it from perishing. "The children ask for bread," say the Holy Scriptures, "and there is no one to break it to them."

Young pupils, sometimes so docile and so desirous of instruction, are like a well-prepared soil; but there is no one to sow the good seed. The parched earth opens to receive the dew of heaven; but the clouds, which ought to extend their fertilizing power, are without water. Apostle of youth, understand well your duties and your dignity; you are a shepherd of souls; you exercise a mission, an apostolate, a divine priesthood. Is not your mission great enough for you to make all possible efforts to discharge it well? Would not your negligence bring lamentable consequences? Does not your generosity give you the right to glorious rewards, sufficient to lead you to discharge holily your sublime duties?

Remember always that religious knowledge is the coin with which souls are bought: to gain them, no price ought to seem too high. There are men in the world who study for the pleasure of science alone, they see only their books, they grow pale over their note-books; the day is not sufficient for their studies, they devote their nights also to them. They wear out their strength and their health in their studies, they break down before their time: and all this, to acquire a little of that empty smoke which is called glory! And for God, for the salvation of souls, to merit an eternal reward, you would fear a little trouble, a little labor! No, it shall not be so with you; you will study the Christian doctrine with all the ardor of which you are capable.

Reproach yourself, as a great fault, with the voluntary loss of a portion of the time for the study of catechism. This time is not yours, it is God's; it belongs to the children whom you ought to instruct, and whom you will, perhaps, leave in ignorance; whom, perhaps, you will not move, nor enlighten, nor strengthen in good; who will lose their salvation on account of your negligence in studying and preparing the catechism !

Ask yourself often how, and in what spirit, you make your study of religion. A negligence in this matter would be soon culpable, and your conscience might be seriously wounded by it.

No illusion, then, on this essential point: it would be too hurtful and dangerous.

You are a member of the community before everything; you would not be a religious, you would give the lie to your most sacred obligations, if you did not force yourself to acquire, and teach with zeal, that sublime doctrine which assures the happiness of those who receive it, and merits for those who dispense it to shine eternally in heaven on thrones of glory.

Important Advice to the Young Catechist.

Oblige yourself to conceive the highest esteem of the office of catechist. Woe to you, if you only attach a secondary importance to it !

How many children, having once left school, hear our holy religion no more spoken of, and will have only the remembrance of the catechism which has been taught them, to preserve them from evil!

Beg God to bless abundantly the work which you are about to undertake. Offer it to him by the hands of Mary. Recommend to him the little children whom he charges you to instruct, and pray to him to give you the qualifications necessary to fulfil this holy mission worthily.

Say to yourself, with a spark of true zeal: Since I am charged with the duty of cultivating a young generation, which will soon be the active part of the parish, I wish to give myself to this work with all the devotedness and application of which I am capable.

Under the influence of this pious thought, make a scruple of the least neglect in the accomplishment of your duty, and do not fail, in the tribunal of penance, to accuse yourself of this negligence, so that your confessor may direct you by his charitable advice on this essential point.

When you are catechising children, you are speaking to understandings hardly opened, for which you must explain each word with perfect clearness, or you will not be understood: now, this cannot be done well without special study. Experience will teach you that it is much more difficult than you imagine to interest children, and to speak to them in a useful way.

Study with extreme care each lesson of the catechism, of which you have to make the explanation. See how you can put it, so as to make it accessible to the minds, so little enlightened as they are, of your little hearers.

See and note what the best works say on each question of the catechism, and ask yourself what you can still add to such explanation, to make it as clear and as practical as possible.

Make a large collection of comparisons, parables, and historical facts, of which you can make use to bring out in relief your catechetical teaching, which, without this, would be dry, abstract, unintelligible, and contradictory.

Speak little, and make them speak much.—If you are a catechist and a great talker, you will be a catechist who is unintelligible and useless. When you have explained a point of doctrine clearly, you ought only to find out if the children understand it; and, to do this, you have no other means than to let them speak, contenting yourself with correcting them when they are wrong; besides, you ought to vary your explanation so as to make them see that they have given a wrong answer: it is through them, as well as through yourself, that the correction must be effected.

Do not make them dwell too much on those questions which are comparatively easy and unimportant. You should always have recourse to this excellent means, not only to gain time, but to give to sluggish minds a facility of grasping the truth. Insist on this in proportion to the importance and difficulty of the subject-matter.

If catechism only consists in a cold and monotonous recital, you will not attract the attention of your pupils, you will not excite their interest, and they will carry away only disgust from a tiresome lesson; you must, therefore, make it pleasant to them, and, to succeed in this, it is necessary, we repeat, to prepare for it with care.

It is not necessary to speak much; you ought not to break out into long explanations, but do not be satisfied with merely asking questions and receiving answers, without making reflections for the children on the truths which you are teaching them. That these little moral reflections may be useful, they should be short, vivid, and inspired by zeal: everything languishes when the heart does not speak. Love and desire earnestly to gain souls, and God, knowing your desires, will give you the necessary qualifications to make your words bring forth fruit.

Remember often that you are not a theologian, and that those whom you have to form are not doctors; avoid, then, everything which might be too high for them or useless.

Do not repeat without discrimination all that you have learned from the books which you have used to prepare your instruction: you must know how to do this, or, at least, confine yourself to certain questions. Depend chiefly on the fundamental truths, the mysteries, sin, and especially on the sacraments.

Always speak with great reserve about sins against the sixth and ninth commandments, and be very prudent in your expressions, lest you should teach the children what they do not know, and give them occasion to ask indiscreet questions.

As much as the intelligence of those whom you have to instruct allows, make them understand how beautiful religion is, and how happy it renders those who practise it:

it is only by making them love it, that you can procure for it faithful children. Yes, it is necessary that the children should find out, of their own accord, that religion is beautiful, lovely, and noble. You labor in vain, if they have a sad and dismal idea of it; and if piety and virtue appear to them under the frightful image of harshness and constraint, while disorder presents itself to them under a pleasant form, all is lost, and you labor in vain.

Why is it that so many young people see in religion something cold, harsh, contradictory, and languishing? It is because no other idea of it has been given them. This has been imposed upon them, and they have never had in their hearts anything open or generous, or anything true, as regards piety and faith.

When God is in question, or religion, or man, or conscience, to strike the imagination, and to correct, is nothing: there must be love.

To give an interest to your catechism, and to leave a lasting impression in the minds of the children, you might relate some edifying historical facts from time to time. When they are short, suited to the subject, and presented in a vivid manner, they can be productive of very great good. But take care of taking indiscriminately everything that you will find in several collections, which are far from presenting an irreproachable choice.

Let there be nothing by chance, nothing trifling, and nothing too long. The Holy Scriptures will supply you with a number of excellent examples. At the end of each of your instructions make a recapitulation, or rather let the children recapitulate the truths which you have explained. Require them to repeat this summary, at the beginning of the next instruction: it is a means of imparting system to your teaching, to connect the different parts, and to oblige the children to be attentive.

Make it a point of honor, or rather a conscientious duty, to make use of all these means, so that your children may never present themselves at the parish catechisms without perfectly knowing the lessons which have been given them by the catechists: the very reputation of your community depends upon this.

Let your pupils learn their catechism well, but, as much as possible, let it be by encouragement. Let the hope of reward, and not the fear of punishment, inspire their efforts. What sad consequences excessive penances, inflicted on incapable or negligent children, may have! They lead too often to hatred of the teacher, of the school, and of religion! Use, then, all care and prudence to avoid such a misfortune. It is particularly for catechism that you ought to employ the means of encouragement which are usual in our classes: compositions, medals, crosses of honor; you can also make use of that excellent reward called *good marks*. These resources, well employed, will be very suitable to excite emulation, a means so fruitful in good results, and without which the object will scarcely ever be attained.

Be kind, be gentle, be patient and merciful, in regard to your young flock: you will be all this, if you love it. You will only be severe, as an exception; and you will only be so, when it is evident that you cannot act otherwise; yet 'return immediately to your amiable gentleness, as the sun reappears in its effulgence, after it has been hidden for a few moments under a light cloud.

To all these means, unite those which your personal experience will furnish you: love your duties, be holily ambitious of fulfilling them well, and God will grant you the grace to become a good catechist.

"What is done through devotedness," says Mgr. Dupanloup, "is done well, and is loved;

by doing it, we are formed, strengthened, and wonderfully exalted ourselves. Everywhere devotedness gathers a hundred-fold of what it does and gives: it increases the strength, and adds to the resources of the mind; it sometimes gives a spirit which does not exist, and always develops that which we have."

Advice on the Way to Give Catechism and to Make the Reflections in a Little Class.

Think often that the salvation of the children depends, in part, on the way in which the catechism and reflection are made to them.

Often give the catechism on the principal mysteries.

Confine yourself to the essential truths, teach little, but well; have recourse to all the means which an enlightened zeal may inspire, so that no pupil may be ignorant of what it is necessary to know in order to be saved.

Return frequently to the same truths, varying the manner of putting the questions, so as to avoid routine.

Avoid all that would be useless, abstract, or beyond the comprehension of the pupils; insist upon the most important and practical points.

Frequently question the children who are less intelligent or attentive: for want of this precaution, you will be exposed to the danger of leaving them in ignorance of things most necessary for salvation.

Give the catechism in a way that is interesting and calculated to make the children love religion; be very encouraging, especially in regard to those who have a difficulty in answering; take in account their good-will, even when they do not answer perfectly well.

Make use of an abridgment of any Diocesan Catechism, or of any good treatise on Christian doctrine.

If the pupils are little advanced, you ought to explain to them the Diocesan Catechism; and, to do this, you must subdivide the questions, explain the words which might not be understood, and give the most essential and practical developments.

The reflection should be simple and familiar: the necessities of those whom you are addressing, should inspire this.

It is especially by apt comparisons and well-chosen details that we can reach the understandings and hearts of little children: you cannot do too much to bring yourself to their level.

Often consult those who can teach you how to perform well these two exercises which are so important and difficult, especially at the beginning.

Examine yourself frequently as to the manner in which you discharge them; ask yourself if you do not lose time, if you make use of the means most suited to obtain the best results.

The young teacher ought especially to pray that God may illuminate him with his light, animate him with his Spirit, and bless the seed of the word which he plants in souls.

Profit by the Occasions which Present themselves to Inculcate the Maxims of Christianity.

"A zealous teacher," says Fr. Judde, "profits by all the means of doing good to his pupils: a number of occasions offer themselves to give them instructions; and the less they seem to be strained, the more fruit they will bring.

"Tragical events have happened in the city, or have been reported in the public journals: you should make some reflections on the judgments of God, always taking care not to insult misfortune, or the memory of any one. One of your scholars is dead or sick, you hear of it, and this can furnish another subject for reflection. 'Be ye always ready: are we?' Another is drowned: 'Oh! if that had happened to any one who is here, in mortal sin!' A child is surprised in a lie—you say a word against liars; a pupil has been distracted in church—a word on the holiness of the place, on the state of our Lord in the sacrifice of the Mass. Your catechism has been on the obligation to study—has any one been negligent? Three days after, you make him repeat what you have said, or you make him say it over again after another: thus is the catechism remembered. If you perceive among your scholars a pressing need of instruction on some point of morality, strive to recall the idea from time to time. Nothing is more suitable for correction than these frequent rehearsals. If you have a difficulty in finding these occasions of speaking of God, it is because you are not sufficiently filled with him: fill yourself still more, it will then flow as from a spring."

INFIDELITY TO THE RELIGIOUS VOCATION.

Weakening of the Esteem of one's Vocation. Its Causes and Consequences.

WHEN the religious spirit grows weak and disappears, we cease to esteem our state of life, we fulfil no longer our duties, except with laxity and negligence; but this is not always a sign of want of vocation. A precious liquor has been put into a beautiful vessel; it is shaken carelessly, a little crack is made; it is not perceptible, perhaps, and yet, although the vessel seems untouched, the liquor escapes, and the vase will soon be empty. The road has been pointed out to a man; he follows it, he begins to walk in it, but, from disgust, weariness, or other cause, he slackens his steps, he stops; it is not a proof that he is not on the right road, but he must recruit his strength, he must ask for nourishment, recall to mind with energy the object in view, and reanimate his courage.

Sometimes the weakening of the religious spirit is the sad consequence of cowardice and idleness; sometimes, too, it is produced by temptations of the enemy of salvation, against whom we are not sufficiently on our guard; it may even be the consequence of a dangerous delusion, that of believing that we are called to a more perfect state of life, to enter into an order, or into a stricter community.

We nurse this idea, we do not speak of it to our director; we make all our little calculations in secret; we examine and exaggerate the petty difficulties which we experience, the distractions of a class, the difficulty of keeping the children in order; we fancy that we shall find an unchangeable calm, an assured happiness, in another position; and, without discerning the snare hidden by the devil, we are troubled and disgusted with our duties; without knowing if we have a real vocation to a more entire retreat, or if we have qualities and means to be received into it, we are disposed to abandon our state of life, and thus we put ourselves in a false position. If you should quit it, what would become of you? How much would this endanger your salvation! But, even if it should not come to this, what a terrible thing is this languor and want of action, which is the consequence of disgust! How much time lost on the way! How much you will be found to have lagged behind the rest!

If, by his own fault, in consequence of his infidelities, a religious loses the spirit of his state of life, what a misfortune! What sad consequences! This disaster does not come like a thunderbolt; it is generally the consequence and punishment of successive infidelities, and has begun by despising little things. But, like a sick man whose senses are dulled little by little, this poor soul reaches a degree of insensibility, which is the proof of the want, or of the loss, of the religious spirit. Nothing touches, nothing moves it; the duties of piety leave it cold and frozen, prayer wearies it, and vocal prayer has no attractions for it. The reception of the sacraments is no longer in its eyes anything but a point of rule; its communions are, at least, lukewarm, if not more than cold. It is a phantom which walks, and still appears, but like one of those fantastic beings which have nothing real about them; in fact, its spirit is elsewhere; it is in the midst of an establishment as a stranger, and takes no interest in anything. Whether the rule is kept or violated, is no matter to such a person. Whether the duties with which he is charged are well or ill done, is all the same to him; whether superiors blame him or not, he pays very little attention. The direction of the children even weighs upon him; he goes to the class as a mere habit, he will let his children be distracted or not, according to his impulse; he will scold them with harshness, but always without troubling himself any more about it. He is like those idols of which the Psalmist speaks: "They have eyes, and see not; ears, and hear not; feet, and walk not." What a sad state! No one can bear it long: a soul cannot live in such languor. To this insensibility, disgust will soon succeed; not only will it be indifferent, but, besides, it will be morose, wearied, and disgusted. The yoke of the rule will become heavy and unbearable, solitude will be its punishment, and the severe restraint in which it must live, will be intolerable. Hitherto this religious loved to remember his happiness; he was happy because he was fervent; now he finds himself unhappy, and he is so in truth. A vague disquiet follows him everywhere, weariness gnaws him, and disgust devours him.

What a sad thing it is for a religious to be disgusted with his state of life! A misfortune for others, as well as for himself! Alas! in spite of the unction of grace, a rule often seems burdensome to him; it is hard for him unceasingly to subjugate his own will, and to obey the sound of the bell which calls him. The sentiment of faith alone can sweeten what is difficult in this; but, when he has not this sentiment of faith, what can he do, what can become of him? Alas! the example, even of his brethren who are faithful, wearies him; their gladness makes him sad; their regularity troubles him; he respects them, and yet repulses them; he loves them, and yet wishes to avoid them.

Sad state of a sick conscience, which cannot bear others nor itself, as a diseased stomach rejects even the most nourishing food! To these ideas are soon joined the remembrance of the world and its pleasures, the regret of one's family, the desire of rest and of freedom from a restraint which has become intolerable. How difficult it is to extricate yourself from such a condition! Oh! use all your efforts to keep it far from you; be faithful, fervent, and generous, and the esteem of your vocation will increase in you, and you will be more and more delighted in your holy state of life, if you fulfil its duties with generosity.

Ingratitude and Danger of a Religious who is Unfaithful to his Vocation.

"God," says St. Liguori, "in calling any one to the religious state, gives him a grace which is not given to everybody: therefore, his indignation must be extreme against all those who despise it. Would not a prince be extremely offended, if, after he had summoned, for an honorable service near his person, one of his poor subjects, through love, and in preference to the lords of his court, this man should refuse the honor through idleness and a false spirit of independence? And do you think that God would not resent such an insult? Ah! he is angry at it, here is his threat: 'Woe to him that gainsayeth his Maker.' (Isa. xlv, 9.) His punishment will begin, even in this life, by the continual disquiet which will attack him; for, says Job: 'Who has resisted him, and has lived in peace?' Then, he will be deprived of those abundant and efficacious graces which are necessary for a holy life. It will be only with great difficulty that he will be able to work out his salvation."

St. Bernard and St. Leo teach the same doctrine. St. Gregory, writing to the Emperor Maurice, who, by an edict, had forbidden his soldiers to become religious, said that it was an unjust law, which closed to many the gates of paradise: for many would be saved in religious life, who would be lost in the world. How many Christians will be condemned at the day of judgment, because they have not been obedient to their vocation! "I have called, and you refused. . . . I also will laugh in your destruction, and will mock when that shall come upon you which you feared." (Prov. i, 24, 26.)

The same saint, writing to some religious who wished to abandon their holy state to return to the world, says: "Pray, reflect before God, and you will return to better feelings: the devil alone can inspire you with the thoughts that fill your minds; for, to wish to renounce the happy state of life in which the mercy of God has placed you, is to wish to renounce your salvation.

"There are many, I say it, and repeat it again, who are lost, because they have lost their vocation. The chain of graces once broken, there are very few resources for these unfortunate persons, whose unfaithfulness is punished even in this world; they are, all their life long, torn with remorse, and a prey to constant disquiets."

The religious, who abandons his holy state,

THE RELIGIOUS VOCATION. 229

not only compromises his temporal happiness, but also his eternal salvation.

"God," says Fr. Lallemant, "attaches to fidelity to our state of life the graces by which he wishes to lead us to heaven: if we are unfaithful to our vocation, he leaves us alone, until, by his mercy, we return to it again."

If it is difficult to be saved in the world, even when God calls us to it, what must it be for those who are there against his holy will?

"The religious who is unfaithful to his vocation, is like a fish out of water; he is like a foolish traveller, who leaves the assured haven of salvation, in order to expose himself to the tempest." (Thomas à Kempis.)

"They that go from thee shall perish." (Ps. lxxii, 27.)

"No man, putting his hand to the plough, and looking back, is fit for the kingdom of God." (Luke ix, 62.)

"He that shall deny me before men, I also will deny him before my Father who is in heaven." (Matt. x, 33.)

Conduct in Temptations against our Vocation.

1. Examine if the thought of abandoning your vocation arises after a communion or a

fervent prayer; see if, on the contrary, it does not take its rise from tepidity, the neglect of your duties, infidelity to grace, some considerable fault, etc.

2. Ask what you would wish to have done at the hour of death; think of the terrible account which must be rendered of a holy vocation, if you have the misfortune to be unfaithful to it.

3. Make known without delay, and with frankness, the temptations against your vocation; do not wait till the evil is past remedy before you discover them to your director.

4. Never act impetuously, under the influence of a lively emotion, or of a strong opposition; but pray, examine seriously, and approach the sacraments with this intention.

5. Check the consequences of an imprudent step. Do not listen to a guilty and blind self-love, which would hinder you from going back to your duty.

6. If the religious state seem too hard, meditate on what Jesus Christ has suffered for us, on the shortness of life, and on the eternal reward.

7. If the pleasures and goods of this world seduce you, oblige yourself to understand the emptiness, the vanity, and the shortness of them.

8. In times of difficulty, read the preceding considerations on the danger of unfaithfulness to your vocation; meditate on the advantages of the religious life, the dangers of the world, the necessity of fulfilling the will of God, the love of Jesus Christ for us, and on your last end.

9. Recall the reasons you had for entering religion, the sentiments which you have experienced there, the dispositions with which you received the habit, etc.

10. Return to your primitive fervor and regularity: we are usually tempted against our vocation, in proportion as we neglect our duties.

11. Pray every day, and thank God for having called you to the religious life; often invoke the Blessed Virgin, St. Joseph, your holy patrons, and your guardian angel, that you may obtain the grace of dying a holy religious.

Say often with the Royal Prophet: "One thing I have asked of the Lord, this will I seek after: that I may dwell in the house of the Lord all the days of my life." (Ps. xxvi, 4.)

Advice of St. Francis of Sales on our Conduct relating to Disgust for our Vocation.

"It is necessary to remain in the boat in which you are, to make the passage from this life to the other, and to remain in it willingly and with love; because, although sometimes we have not been put there by the hand of God, but by the hand of man, nevertheless, when we are once in it, God wills that we should remain, and, consequently, remain quietly and willingly.

"Let us beware of going out of it: 'There is no mean between your departure and your destruction.'

"If you wish to do well, consider as a temptation everything which suggests to you a change of place; for, while your mind looks elsewhere than where it is, you will never succeed in doing well what must be done where you are. This point is of such importance to your soul, that I would write it willingly in my blood.

"There is no vocation which has not its disgusts, its irksomeness, and its trials.

"Whoever is not fully resigned, but turned hither and thither, will never have rest. Those who have fever find no place which is agreeable. They have not stayed a quarter of an hour in one bed when they wish to be in another: it is not the bed which is the cause of this, but the fever which torments them everywhere.

"Our Lord wills that we renounce ourselves, that is, our own will. I should like this or that, I should be better here or there: these are temptations. Our Lord knows full well what he is doing: let us do what he wishes, let us remain where he has placed us.

"How should we testify our love for him who has suffered so much for us, if not by submitting cheerfully to our dislikes, repugnances, and contradictions? We must thrust our heads amid the thorns of difficulties, and let our hearts be pierced with the lance of contradiction; we must drink the gall and swallow the vinegar, and, lastly, we must eat wormwood and bitterness, because God wills it.

"Lastly, since you have hitherto nourished and cherished the temptation in your heart, now, with all your heart, you must nourish and strengthen this resignation to the will of God in trials, tribulations, etc. If you should find any difficulty on this point, do not change anything until you have considered eternity, and have placed yourself in holy indifference, and have taken the advice of some worthy servant of God; for the enemy, seeing you victorious over this temptation, by your resignation to the divine will, will make use of all kinds of expedients to trouble you.

"Treat this temptation as you would treat the temptations of blasphemy, treason, heresy, or despair; do not entertain it, do not reason, do not listen to it; oppose it as much as you can, by frequent protestations of fidelity even until death."

Extract from the "Letter of St. Francis of Sales."

"Say with the Psalmist: 'Lord, thou art the God of my heart, and my inheritance forever' (Ps. lxxii, 26); and with St. Paul: 'Who, then, shall separate us from the love of Christ? Shall tribulation, or distress . . . or danger . . . or the sword ? . . . Neither death, nor life . . . nor things present, nor things to come . . . nor height, nor depth, nor any other creature, shall be able to separate us from the love of God.'" (Rom. viii, 35–39.)

OF THE VOWS.

Excellence of the Vows.

THE three vows of poverty, chastity, and obedience, constitute the substance of the religious state; they make it a state of perfection. Perfection, in fact, consists in extinguishing the triple concupiscence, which is, as it were, a furnace of sin in us, and in renouncing all the goods which could lead us away from God, in order to attach ourselves irrevocably to him. Now, this is exactly what the religious soul does by the vows. By the vow of poverty, it renounces material goods, and deprives cupidity of its nourishment. By the vow of chastity, it renounces the pleasures of the sense, and overcomes the concupiscence of the flesh. Lastly, by the vow of obedience, it renounces the dearest of all its goods, the independence of the will, and thus subdues even the most invincible of all concupiscences, viz., pride, the source of all vice.

These vows, then, constitute the most perfect of all sacrifices: they are a complete holocaust, by which the creature sacrifices itself without reserve to the Creator. Moreover, by the profession, this holocaust is not a passing homage, it is not the work of a day: it lasts as long as life, or, rather, it embraces all eternity. It is the true perpetual sacrifice, of which every instant in the life of a religious ought to be the renewal; it is the irrevocable donation made to God, of everything which it has pleased him to leave in the power of our liberty. If, then, sacrifice is the great end of our earthly existence, and the principal means which we have of glorifying God and of attaining eternal happiness, without doubt the vows of religion are the most efficacious of all the instruments of salvation, and the most excellent, the most certain, and the most profitable of all the ways which can lead us to perfection.

But what enhances still more the holiness of the religious profession is that it is, of all states of life, the one which makes us more like to Jesus Christ crucified. In fact, the sacrifice of this divine Saviour on the cross was nothing else but a perfect renunciation of the three kinds of goods of which the religious despoils himself by the three vows. It is not, then, without reason that these vows have been compared to the three nails by which our divine Master was fastened to the cross. It would, doubtless, be a very glorious martyrdom, and one much to be desired for a Christian, to be fastened to the cross of his God with the same nails which pierced his hands and feet. This is the happiness of the religious. His profession brings him nearer to Jesus crucified than all the material instruments which deprived the body of the man-God of life could ever do. The true cross of our Saviour is his renunciation; it is on this holy cross that every religious is nailed in his turn, as on an altar on which the divine Lamb is to remain even to the end of the world; it is there that he receives, by means of the three vows, the death of the soul, which makes him live the risen life of Jesus Christ. The religious profession is then, by the same title as baptism and martyrdom, the reproduction, in the Christian, of the death of Jesus Christ. Thus the holy doctors do not hesitate to declare that, when it is made with a sincere heart, and with an entirely determined will, it participates in the privileges which baptism and martyrdom impart, of purifying the soul from all its stains, and of blotting out from the book of divine justice all the debts which it would have had to pay in purgatory.

The Vows Render the Works of a Religious far more Meritorious.

St. Thomas gives three principal reasons for this, which Rodriguez explains as follows:

First reason.—Religion, being the most excellent of all moral virtues, by regulating what we do for the service of God, gives a special merit to the acts which it produces. The vows are evidently an act of religion, since, after martyrdom, they are the greatest and the noblest sacrifice which a creature can offer to the Creator. It follows hence, that the vows enhance the value of all the acts of virtue which accompany it, by making them become acts of religion, that is to say, holy things consecrated to God. These works have a double merit: that of the virtue which they contain, and that of the act of religion. Thus, chastity, poverty, and obedience have first their intrinsic merit as virtues, then a second merit as acts of religion; so that we merit more when we act out of obedience to the vows, than by doing good of our own pure inclination. This truth will be better understood by reasoning from the contrary. As a religious, who sins against chastity, commits two sins—one against the sixth commandment, and the other against the vow which he has made; so a religious, who faithfully keeps the vow of chastity, has two kinds of merit—that of observing the commandment of God, and that of fulfilling his vow; and this latter, being a pure act of religion, is of far greater price and value than the former.

Second Reason.—To act in virtue of a vow is to give our actions a new merit, which is measured by the offering which we make to God. What is the offering which the religious makes to God? He not only offers him what he does, but also the impossibility in which he has placed himself of doing otherwise; and he offers him his liberty, which is the greatest sacrifice that he can make him: he gives to God the tree with the fruit. As he who gives the tree with the fruit gives much more than he, who, giving the fruit, keeps the tree for himself; so the religious offers far more to God than do even virtuous persons who live in the world. These last give the fruit of the tree—that is to say, their good works; but they keep the tree, that is, the liberty of disposing of themselves, and of acting as it shall suit them. The religious, on the contrary, gives himself entirely to God—he gives the tree and the fruit; he gives him his actions, words, thoughts, will, and liberty; in a word, he gives him everything, so that he keeps nothing for himself, and nothing more remains for him to offer. St. Bonaventure makes use of another comparison, and says that as he who surrenders the entire ownership of a thing, gives more than he who only lends it; so a religious, who consecrates himself to God by vows, gives far more than seculars who do not consecrate themselves to him in this way. The secular only lends himself, as it were, to God; whereas a religious, by giving his will, his liberty, and his actions, gives himself entirely to God.

Third Reason.—The goodness of our actions does not depend on the beauty with which they shine in the eyes of men, but only on the will which produces them. The more perfect the will is, the more perfect will be the works which it produces. Now, it is very certain that the more firmness and constancy there is in the will, the more perfect it is; because, with these dispositions, it is further removed from all evil, and is more fit to work with that courage and perseverance which are regarded as the essential conditions of virtue. Although it is not uncommon to meet in the world with wills which resist the attraction to evil, and which practise virtue with admirable constancy, it is, nevertheless, indisputable that this constancy is infallibly acquired by the vows, which give a great stability in virtue to the religious who has made them with good dispositions, and who observes them faithfully. From these principles, it cannot be denied that the good actions of a religious are of a perfection so much the higher, and of a merit so much the greater, as they proceed from a more firm and constant will.

The result of this doctrine is that the religious, who is faithful to his vows, reaps the most abundant merits, even in the most trivial things. Whatever, then, may be the duties which you have to fulfil; whatever may be the labors in which you are engaged, if you act from obedience, your works, we are not afraid to repeat it, will always have the merit attached to the practice of good, and, besides, the merit attached to the observance of the vows. If a workman, who is paid double wages, devotes himself with so much zeal to his masters interests, what ought not your ardor to be, and your fidelity in observing the vows, which secure you so many merits? Penetrate yourself with this truth, which, well considered, will fill you with a courage above every trial, in the midst of the labors and sacrifices which the strict observance of your vows demands of you.

Let the thought of these precious advantages inspire you with an ardent desire of binding yourself to our Lord by vows, if you have not that happiness yet, and lead you to regulate your conduct so well, that you may make yourself worthy of that favor.

The Vows are a Valuable Help against Inconstancy.

The vows, far from destroying or weakening the liberty, purify and perfect it, on the contrary, by strengthening it in good, and by fortifying it against the seductions of evil.

"Look," says St. Ignatius, in his celebrated letter on Obedience,—"look upon it as the supreme good of your free-will that you are able to give it back entirely into the hands of Him who has given it to you, by depriving yourself of it in appearance. In this way, you do not lose it, you perfect it; for you conform it to the supreme rule of perfection, the will of God, whose interpreter and vicegerent is your superior. Liberty does not consist in the power of sinning: sin is not a mark of strength, but of weakness. The power of doing evil is nothing else but the power of evil over him who gives himself up to it; and this power is in direct opposition to the power which he has to commit it. Liberty is benefited by everything which destroys this terrible power; and the more this is lessened, the more the other is increased and perfected."

This is precisely the effect of the vows, in that they make perfection a kind of necessity. Happy necessity, says St. Augustine, which imposes upon us the obligation of tending always toward what is better! Do not regret that you are bound by the vows, but rejoice, on the contrary, that you are deprived of a liberty which you could not use, except to your detriment. If any one were to see you walking on the road to a precipice, would it not be doing you a signal favor to close up the road, and so make it impossible for you to destroy yourself? Now, if ever you are lost, it will be the exclusive work of your own will, for, if there is a hell, says St. Bernard, it is only because self-will exists. The more narrow the way of your will is, the broader and smoother is the way to happiness; and thus, far from losing your free-will by subjecting it, by the vow of obedience, to that of a superior, you only make it stronger and more perfect, by placing it under the obligation of being constantly conformed to the will of God.

How many religious will owe their perseverance and salvation to the vows which they had the happiness of pronouncing! How many, in the midst of weariness, temptations, and seductive occasions, would have been unfaithful, if they had not contracted these precious obligations, which have supported their weakness, and have made them triumph over their natural inconstancy!

To a Religious who has had the Happiness of Making his Vows.

You have made the oblation of yourself to the Lord: we say to you with Rodriguez, do not take back your gift. You have renounced all the things of the earth: beware of resuming the pursuit of anything which you have once and forever banished from your desires. You have renounced riches: beware of attaching yourself to anything in religion, for, what would it profit you to have despoiled yourself of all that you had in the world, if you wish to possess the least thing in religion? You have renounced your own will and your own judgment: take care of thinking even of this with regret! You have renounced all pleasures, all the vain joys of the world, and the satisfactions of the flesh: beware of letting them invade your soul anew! Be not such a fool as to build up again what you have destroyed: this would be to prevaricate and to look back, after you have put your hand to the plough.

Consider, therefore, that you no longer belong to yourself but to God, to whom you have done homage with all that is in you, and that is yours; and so take care not to claim anything in the world. It would be dishonest to wish to dispose of anything against the will of him to whom it belongs. By the act of your religious consecration, you have given to God the tree with the fruit. What should we say of any one who, having given a tree to another to be planted in his garden, should go afterward and gather the fruit? Would he not be considered as appropriating the goods of another? And this is precisely what the religious does who desires to follow his own will, instead of giving himself up in all things to the guidance of obedience. He does much worse: by appropriating a thing consecrated to God, he renders himself guilty of a sacrilege, which is an abomination in the eyes of the Lord, as he himself declares in strong terms in Isaias: "I am the Lord who love justice, and abhor rapine in a holocaust." Can you imagine a crime more horrible than that of taking something away from a holocaust offered to God without reserve? There is not a greater crime, says St. Bernard, than to wish to arrogate to one's self the least right over a will which has been once sacrificed to the Lord.

It is thus that, stimulating your heart by these and other like considerations, you should exert yourself to correspond with the grace of predilection with which God has deigned to favor you, by permitting you to consecrate yourself to him by vows. If you look at the burden of the task, look also at the value of the reward. "We have promised great things," said St. Francis of Sales to his religious, "but far greater still have been promised to us." Be faithful, therefore, to your promises, and keep your eyes and heart fixed upon those that have been made to you.

Of the Annual Renovation of Vows.

Virtue and perfection are very difficult to our degenerate nature; sin, by corrupting it, has inflicted so deep a wound in its original powers for good, and has developed so violent an inclination to evil, that, whatever may have been our fervor at the beginning, we always experience a fatal tendency to relax, and to return soon to our former tepidity. Like the weights of a clock, which always drag downward, our flesh, which, in its origin and nature, belongs to the earth, unceasingly tends to draw us toward the earth. When, yielding to this sad attraction, we have had the misery to start aside, and even to fall, it is necessary that we should have something to help us to rise up again.

Nothing is more fitted to produce this happy result than the solemn renovation of vows, which is made every year.

That this ceremony, commemorative of your religious consecration, may be a means of reanimating your piety, and a powerful incitement to devote yourself with new vigor to the accomplishment of the duties of your vocation, you must prepare yourself for it in the most serious way.

In order to attain more certainly the end which you should propose to yourself in the renovation of vows, it is a good thing to make use of the following means:—

Make a *novena*, or at least a *triduum*, to prepare yourself for this important action.

During this time, without in any way changing your occupations, make your whole day a continual preparation for this great action; fulfil all your duties in a spirit of renovation; let your meditations, holy Mass, your spiritual reading, and examens, be directed to this end.

As is the practice in a large number of communities, make a general confession of the last year before the renovation.

Examine your conduct seriously, and give an exact and detailed account of it. It will be necessary, in regard to the vow of poverty, to examine if you do not seek your own ease, if you do not dispose of anything without permission, if you do not keep certain objects which are not necessary, nor truly useful. With regard to the vow of chastity, you must examine if you have not an inordinate affection for any creature, if you do not allow yourself or desire any sensual pleasure. As regards the vow of obedience, you must examine whether you have not a too great attachment to your own will and judgment. With regard to the vow of teaching gratuitously, you will ask yourself whether you have accepted anything from your pupils or their parents; you will especially examine whether you discharge your duty with zeal, and whether you use all your efforts to form good Christians.* Lastly, you must consider all the faults which you have committed against the observance of your vows, you must weigh their gravity, and excite yourself to a deep contrition for having violated, or discharged with negligence, obligations so solemn and sacred.

In making your renovation, you ought not only to grieve over the past which recalls to mind so many negligences, and perhaps even infidelities; you should especially look forward to the future, so as to order it in a manner suited to your needs.

If you can satify yourself that you have been faithful to your obligations, in this case resolve to make fresh progress in the ways of perfection. But if you find, in your past conduct, habits which are contrary to your vocation, you must absolutely determine to use every effort to correct yourself for the future.

The essential effect which the renovation of vows should produce in you, is a perfect renewal. This renewal consists in reviving

---

* For this examination you can use the questions which are to be found in the " Monthly Retreat," page 119; you can also, before the renovation, read and meditate seriously on the considerations which members of a community ought to make from time to time, regarding their state of life and employment

in your soul the sentiments of fervor which inflamed it on the solemn day of your first consecration. Then you should give yourself to God without reserve, you should renounce everything which might turn you aside from your vocation, and you should submit to all the sacrifices which the sanctification of your soul requires. To be perfect, your renewal ought to put you in the same dispositions. You must renounce, not only some habits, but *all* without exception; you must make an absolute and entire sacrifice of yourself; you must give yourself to God without reserve, and as long as your vows shall last; and it is necessary that this renewal should operate in your mind by purity of intention, in your heart by a true detachment, and in your conduct by the holiness of your actions. To say all in one word, this renewal must be interior and exterior, entire and continual.

Take all possible precautions, so that every year it may be thus with you.

How Profitable it is to Renew our Vows.

Beside the solemn renovation of vows, it is good for every religious to renew frequently, in private, the sacred obligations which he has had the happiness of contracting. To renew vows in this way is not to contract fresh obligations, but only to renew the remembrance of those already made, and to ratify them by a new act of the will. It is to reiterate an act, fulfilled before, and to confirm it joyfully, with the intention of testifying to God that, far from feeling the least regret at the sacrifice, we feel that we are not able to thank him sufficiently for having vouchsafed to accept it; that, if it were not already consummated, we would be quite ready to make it; that we wish we had still a thousand worlds to leave, and a thousand hearts to offer, in order to make a new holocaust. Accomplished in this spirit, it has a merit proportionate to that of the first act. Taking pleasure in a sin committed is a fresh sin, and a new reason for punishment; pleasure in a good action of our past life is also a new act of virtue, which pleases God, and a new title for his reward.

St. Francis Xavier considered this practice so salutary, that he advised its daily use. According to him, it is impossible for a religious to find a more powerful weapon against every kind of temptation; and he advised all to fortify themselves with it every morning and evening, at the end of their prayers.

If your fervor has not yet attained the height of so holy a practice, adopt, at least, that of some who make it a rule to renew their vows every time that they approach the holy table, and, during their thanksgiving, to ask of themselves an account of the manner in which they observe them, to subject their conscience to a severe examination on this matter, and to excite themselves to fulfil their obligations with greater fidelity.*

To a Young Religious who is Preparing for the First Vows.

The excellence of the vows, and the precious advantages which they procure, ought to inspire you with the desire of forming these sacred engagements as soon as possible.

Before doing this, instruct yourself thoroughly in the obligations which you propose to contract. Penetrate yourself deeply with the extent and force of the engagements

---

* Many fervent souls have the salutary custom of renewing their religious vows when they say the Angelus, which furnishes an easy occasion. To honor the Word conceived by the Holy Ghost, they renew the vow of chastity; to unite themselves to Mary, saying, "Be it done to me according to thy word," they renew the vow of obedience; and to honor the humiliations of "the Word made flesh," they renew the vow of poverty.

which you are about to make. It is necessary for a religious to understand clearly to what he is bound by the vows. A vow must not be confounded with many resolutions which we make before God, even under the form of a promise, the object of which is to make us serve him better. That it may be truly a vow, we must have the intention of engaging in it under pain of sin.

A vow being an act of supreme worship, which is due to God alone, and a true contract with the Divine Majesty itself, a religious ought to understand how sacred and inviolable this bond is; and how this engagement, once contracted, requires us to banish even every thought of inconstancy.

We are not obliged to bind ourselves by vow; but, once that we have done so, we are bound, under pain of mortal sin, to keep the engagements which we have contracted. "If thou hast vowed anything to God, defer not to pay it; for an unfaithful and foolish promise displeaseth him; . . . and it is much better not to vow than, after a vow, not to perform the thing promised." (Eccles. v, 3, 4.) In the second place, consult your own strength, and prepare yourself in a fitting manner for so sacred an action.

You should reflect and examine seriously

if you will be able, with the assistance of grace, to fulfil the engagements which you wish to contract. In circumstances so important, do not act of yourself, but consult your superiors, and especially your confessor; and faithfully follow their counsels.

If, in their wisdom, your superiors advise you to defer your petition, or if the chapter put you off for a time, submit with humility; do not complain of these decisions, which are made for your good, but correct your faults; and, when the time shall have come, repeat your petition.

When you know that you will be admitted to make your vows, bless the Lord for it; think often of the happiness which you will have in consecrating yourself to God; pray so that you may obtain all the graces which are necessary for you to keep your engagements well.

Prepare the victim, so that it may be offered, pure and without spot, upon the altar of sacrifice.

Hasten with your desires the moment in which you will be able to give yourself to the Lord.

Purify your intention; let no human motive induce you to make so holy a step; never let the desire of the esteem of men, nor the fear of displeasing them, the interest of your own reputation, nor any other motive inspired by vanity, ambition, or nature, lead you to make or renew your vows. To obey such culpable sentiments would be to outrage the Lord, to lose the merits of your consecration, and to drive far from you the special graces without which you would never be able to keep your sacred obligations.

Prepare yourself carefully, but without fear or anxiety, for the examination which you must submit to before making your vows; make stronger efforts to penetrate yourself with the spirit of the matter on which you will be questioned, than in being able to retain the mere letter of it.

When the moment for pronouncing your vows shall have come, prepare yourself more directly, by making, as perfectly as possible, your annual retreat. Make yourself feel the necessity of renewing yourself in reality. Let the time of your first obligations be for you a starting-point of a new life; let the day on which you pronounced your vows be always very dear to you; and never cease to look upon it as one of the most glorious days of your life.

After having pronounced your vows, consider yourself as the property of God; only live to please him; devote yourself generously to his interests; take seriously to heart those beautiful words, pronounced after communion in presence of the Blessed Sacrament: "To procure thy glory as much as shall be possible for me, and as thou shalt demand of me."

To a person consecrated to the Lord by vows, may be fitly applied the beautiful words of St. Bernard: "A religious is a living vessel, which should contain Jesus Christ."

You may now say: "In the simplicity of my heart I have joyfully offered all these things to thee, O my God!" (1 Par. xxix, 17.)

And the angels reply: "Ye are not your own; .... glorify and bear God in your body." (1 Cor. vi, 19, 20.)

No, you are not your own, for you have taken upon you the yoke of the Lord.

Let Christians content themselves with giving the Lord the use of their body and soul; but, for a religious, it is a duty to give him all that he has, and all that he is. He should say often, with St. Ignatius: "Receive, O Lord! all my liberty, my memory, my understanding, and all my will; all that I have, and all that I possess, thou hast given it unto me: I give it wholly to thee, and I submit to the direction of thy will. Give me thy love and thy grace alone: I shall be rich enough, and I desire nothing more."

Of the Merit of our Good Works, and of the Application which we can Make of them.

We are going to offer to you, under this head, several considerations taken from Fr. P. Cotel, which, if well understood, cannot but be very profitable to you.

1. Let us lay it down as a principle that the source of merit, in relation to the eternal reward, is charity, and not precisely the pain or difficulty overcome; although it is true to say that effort and suffering are generally the mark and proof of the greatest charity.

Thus, for instance, the martyrs had, doubtless, great merit in suffering for Jesus Christ, but the most holy Virgin merited more than all of them in the least acts of her life, although there was not always suffering.

Here is a practical truth, which offers a full direction: it is the clear interpretation of that sentence of St. Augustine: "Love, and do what you wish."

Here are two others, which are connected with it; and these three truths, while showing us what pleases God more in our devotions, have also some consolation for us when it is not given to us to do for him as much as we should wish.

2. The merit of a good work lies much more in the goodness of the intention which animates us, than in the material act itself; and God regards the quantity less than the quality of the things which are offered to him.

3. The most meritorious intention is that which, on one hand, is more free from all alloy, and, on the other, proposes a more perfect motive for action. If, therefore, we wish to merit more, we must not only banish every bad intention, but also every motive which is imperfect, and suggested by nature; then we must make the most perfect intention the motive of our actions. Now, this is evidently that which has directly in view the glory of God. It is true that the motive of our own good, when it is according to God, and in the supernatural order especially, contains, implicitly or interpretatively, the intention of the glory of God; but when this is formal, it is of far greater value, as it proceeds from pure charity. If these intentions are explicit, they may serve to strengthen each other; and we are sometimes obliged to unite them in this manner, to help us to fulfil our duty in difficult cases. Still, it is

more perfect in itself to abstract from one's own good, and, by a certain act of the will, to throw one's self far beyond our thought and our affection toward God, the only good.

Besides, it is impossible not to feel, although without reflecting on it, that he will think of our good; for, in doing a service to a friend, my only thought is to wish him well; but my heart tells me that I may depend on him. And this is eminently true in the service of God; for this friend, who is infinitely good, has willed that our interests should be inseparably united to his glory.

4. Our good works, preëminently those which God wishes and accepts before all others, are the works of our vocation, whether the rule and obedience prescribe them for ourselves, or whether they go, according to the order, to the salvation of souls. It would be a great delusion to leave or neglect what duty prescribes, to undertake other works, however good and holy they might be.

5. In a good action three kinds of merits are distinguished:—

The first is that of the *work itself*, by virtue of which, what good we do in a state of grace, and with a pure intention, is worth a degree of glory for us in heaven.

The second is that of *impetration*, which obtains us new assistance and other graces, which we desire from our Lord; it is a true prayer, for prayer itself is nothing else but the interpreter of the desire.

The third merit is that of *satisfaction*, which serves to pay our debts to the divine justice: every good work, in fact, supposes some labor and effort here below, and so takes a character of penance.

What we call the merit of a work remains always to him who has done it, and cannot be transferred to another; the two other kinds of merits, that of impetration and that of satisfaction, are generally transferable,— that is, you can apply them to others in this world, or to the souls in purgatory.

When you pray or do any other good work, with the intention of obtaining something for yourself, if the thing is in the order of salvation, you will infallibly be heard, says St. Thomas, if not immediately, at least at the moment which is best for you. And it is equally true that the satisfactory merit of your good works, when you offer them for yourself, is always accepted by God. But it is not entirely the same with the prayers which you offer for another's intention, or with the satisfaction which you wish to apply to him.

To excite this Christian charity, you must add a fervent and persevering prayer to obtain more victorious graces, which will end by triumphing over the obstinate sinner. Indulgences, in particular, are not applicable to the souls in purgatory, except by way of *suffrage*, that is, of intercession or oblation; and although we know, through holy Church, that God accepts them generally, nevertheless, he has not expressly promised this: and he may have just reasons, in certain cases, for not applying them according to our prayer. Besides, there are indulgences granted only to those who gain them: such are those which the Sovereign Pontiff has not formally declared to be applicable to the faithful departed.

6. How ought we to apply the impetratory and satisfactory merits of our good works?

First, it is evident that the distribution of our spiritual alms demands order and a suitable diligence. Avoid, then, following your inclination at haphazard, without determining anything, and without any charity or zeal in the detail of your works of piety. Learn early not to allow so many things, of which you might make so good a use, to be wasted and lost. Make a habit of applying specially your beads, Masses, communions, penances.

etc.: an explicit application is always worth more than vague generalities.

How many necessities demand your charity in the Church militant and suffering! Think of those of your parents, benefactors, and friends: it is the best proof that you can give them of your gratitude and affection. Occupy yourself often with your spiritual family, with the needs of the entire community, of your superior, and of your pupils.

You have to ask for success in matters which relate to the glory of God, to the exaltation of holy Church, to the conversion of sinners, heretics and infidels. It is an act of justice for you to remember to sustain in their labors the apostles who are employed for the salvation of souls throughout the earth; besides, too, you will thus have a share in the merit of their good works.

There are some who place all their merits, beforehand, in the hands of the Blessed Virgin, begging her to make the distribution of them, either to the living or to the dead. This practice is holy, provided it does not encourage the negligence and carelessness of which we spoke above. These two methods may be united, by making our own petitions surbordinate to the will of the divine mother: most certainly God, who has established her as the general treasurer of his goods, will be pleased if we imitate his example.

Of Practices of Devotion.

Devotional practices do not constitute the substance of piety; but they are the natural fruit of it, and the nourishment more or less necessary for it. You cannot, therefore, dispense yourself from adopting a certain number of these practices, which you will choose among those which are the most excellent in themselves, and which are best adapted to your taste and position.

These practices will serve to nourish in you the spirit of faith, and make you "walk before God and become perfect." They will have the special result of keeping up your fervor in your exercises of obligation; for, it is matter of experience that those who embrace them are they who make their meditations, examens, spiritual reading, and communions, the best.

Let us add another consideration: it is, that the mind requires some relaxation if we do not wish it to be weakened, and wear the body by a too continued activity. Now, piety itself, which is "profitable for all things," as the apostle says, knows very well itself how to give these necessary rests; and it is from it especially that the good religious loves to ask for these moments of relaxation, which are so useful for regaining strength.

The consideration of what others do ought not to lead you to follow this or that practice, any more than it would be a reason to omit them; although, assuredly, it is very praiseworthy to follow a good example, just as charity may also sometimes justly recommend an omission.

Every one should see, with the advice of his director, what is suited for himself; for grace does not require the same measure from all: it may lead this one to this practice, and that one to another. Just as characters are different, so are the impulses of a good soul, and we may apply here what St. Paul says: "Let not him that eateth, despise him that eateth not; and he that eateth not, let him not judge him that eateth. . . . Let every man abound in his own sense." (Rom. xiv, 3, 5.)

But one thing should be avoided by all, and that is: to oppose a studied resistance to the Holy Spirit. There may be carelessness, indevotion, and a sort of dulness, in some souls; and this is an evil which is very often manifested in proportion to the natural activity which is exhibited everywhere in other matters. When the passion for study, or an ill-regulated zeal for one's employment, has frozen the heart, it does not wish any longer to do anything of its own accord for the service of God. When knowledge is esteemed more than piety, we despise what we have hitherto valued, and we become like those worldly Christians who, while they insist that it is enough to do what is of obligation, neglect to do well even that which is essential.

On the other hand, it is possible that it may be necessary to say to some of us: Avoid multiplying your devotions too much; pious persons in the world can often do what is not possible in religious life, because other duties prevent it. In the world, you had certain practices, which did you good, and which, perhaps, were necessary for you: usually these same practices are not suited to religious life, or, at least, you have found better in the means which it presents to you. This is why, when you enter into religion, the Church takes away the obligations which have been previously contracted, even by vows.

Of the Way in which a Religious should Practise Special Devotions.

There are many who imagine that long prayers, numerous mortifications, and such things, are the indispensable foundation and principal element of a devotion; so that they do not think they can undertake any, unless they have much leisure, and if they do not multiply special practices. This is a mistake; and we religious particularly, whose time is always filled up with occupations assigned by obedience, ought to know that, notwithstanding our work, it is still very easy to practise these special devotions. Here is the method which I propose that you should follow. I suppose, for example, that you wish to make a *novena*, a *triduum*, etc., either in common with your brethren for a general need, or in private for your own personal necessity, to remove a difficulty, to overcome a temptation, to obtain a virtue, to beg a conversion, etc. Doubtless, it is right to choose some extraordinary exterior practice, which gives the mark and special feature to this devotion. It may be, for instance, a prayer which you will recite with an increase of confidence and fervor; and you may join to it, to make it more efficacious, some suitable mortification. You will thus have, as it were, the material part of your devotion. But what will be the essence and soul of it, which is, consequently, the most excellent part of it? Without changing anything in your occupations, you will, in a manner, impregnate your whole day with it; your intentions will lead you to it, in all that you have to do, in study, in class, in recreation, etc.; you will unite with it your meditation, holy Mass, your visits to the Blessed Sacrament, your spiritual reading, and examens. If there should be a victory to gain over yourself, a disgust to overcome, a sensuality to avoid, or an inclination to vanity, impatience, or levity to repress, these will be so many good chances which you will hasten to embrace. This is an excellent way of practising a devotion. I advise you to prefer it to every other; for it is truly that which will bring down upon you the favor which you wish to obtain.

Of Indulgences.

Indulgences are the fruit of the passion and death of Jesus Christ, the fruit of the merits and sorrows of Mary, and of the penance and martyrdom of the saints. They purify our souls from the remnants of sin, by discharging our debts to the Divine Majesty; they lead us to live constantly in the state of sanctifying grace, and to practise works of charity, piety, and Christian mortification; they shorten for us the severe sufferings of the other life, or even preserve us from them entirely; in fine, they are a most excellent means in our hands to relieve the souls of our relations, brethren, and benefactors, who may be suffering in the fires of purgatory, and to hasten their entrance into the abode of eternal joy, light, and peace. Would it not be to do an injury to God's goodness and to the tenderness of the Church; would it not be a cruelty to ourselves and to our friends, if we were to neglect so salutary a gift?

"For those who are seeking the love of God and heaven," says St. Ignatius, "indulgences are a rich treasure, and, as it were, so many precious stones; they are worthy of such great esteem, that I find myself utterly unable to praise them suitably. For the sake of the love and respect which you owe to God, I exhort you all to have a great esteem for the grace which is given to you by the granting of indulgences."

All the faithful, and, with greater reason, every religious, ought to be zealous in gaining the indulgences of the Church.

Nevertheless, I think it useful to remark that, even in the best things, there must be discretion and a suitable moderation. Those who might imagine that everything ought to give way to—I know not what kind of eagerness in gaining indulgences, would find themselves greatly deceived. If the Church has multiplied them with a motherly liberality, it is not precisely so that each of her children should set to work to gain all of them; which, indeed, would be impossible. She wished only to give them every facility to come and draw upon her treasures; but they would act contrary to her intention and to true piety, who, under pretence of gaining more indulgences, should neglect their duties, and embarrass themselves with endless practices. Besides, the merit of a good work, inasmuch as it makes us pleasing to God, is of a much higher order, and, consequently, more worthy of our zeal, than the simple merit of *satisfaction;* and, in fact, the indulgences which the Church grants, are only means which she makes use of to move the faithful to perform works of sanctification, properly so-called.

After these observations, the object of which is, certainly, not to turn you aside from a devotion so legitimate, let us recall to mind this undoubted truth, viz.: that the indulgences, peculiar to the community, ought to be most cherished by you; in fact, since they are granted in view of the services which it has rendered, and still renders to the Church, would they not come to you with a fulness and efficacy altogether special, by virtue of the merits of the entire community?

Of Ejaculatory Prayers.

Prayers, which are called *ejaculatory*, are holy impulses, lively affections, and ardent desires, by which our souls are raised toward God. They are short prayers, the practice of which is easy, and the fruit most excellent. These kinds of aspirations, says St. Francis of Sales, supply, in çase of necessity, all others, but all others cannot replace them. They can be made at all times, in every place, and in the midst of every kind of employment.

"In this way," says Fr. Faber, "we can sigh for the glory of God, send up into heaven, like an arrow of love, some words in the interest of Jesus Christ, or murmur a short prayer, in whatever place we may be. Without wearying ourselves, we can make a number of these ejaculatory prayers during the day, and each of them is greater in the eyes of God than a battle gained, a scientific discovery, or a political revolution. To many of these prayers an indulgence is attached; thus, a short phrase alone will serve us to acquire merits, to obtain graces, to satisfy for our sins, to glorify God, to give homage to Jesus and Mary, to convert sinners, and to relieve the sufferings of the souls in purgatory.

"Can we do nothing more for Jesus than what we have done up to this very day? O Love! it is for you to teach us what we ought to do, and to remind us of it when we forget it."

The Apostleship of Prayer.

"I desire, first of all, that supplications, prayers, intercessions, and thanksgivings be made for all men. ... For this is good and acceptable in the sight of God our Saviour, who will have all men to be saved, and to come to the knowledge of the truth." (1. Tim. ii, 1-4.)

To suffer for the salvation of souls, to pray for the salvation of souls, is the apostleship which God proposes to all generous hearts which wish to glorify him and to acquire for themselves the immortal glory of having extended the kingdom of God, and saved mankind, their brethren.

If you are not called to the apostleship of the word and action, you can exercise that of prayer and sacrifice: an apostleship humble and barren in the eyes of men, but glorious and fruitful before God.

Your lot is beautiful; it is the lot of Jesus, Mary, and Joseph:—

It is the lot of Jesus.—This divine Saviour, having come down upon earth to preach the gospel to the nations, devoted thirty years of his life to the hidden apostleship of immolation and prayer, and only three years to the apostleship of the word and action.

And from all ages, and now and even to the end of the world, what in heaven and what on earth is the apostleship of our Saviour? The apostleship of sacrifice and prayer. In heaven, the adorable heart and mouth of Jesus Christ speak to God the Father for the salvation of the world. And on earth, what does this same heart do? It intercedes, prays, offers itself, and sacrifices itself, day and night, and every instant of the day and night, in a thousand tabernacles, and on a thousand altars, for the salvation of the world.

The lot of Mary.—It was the prayer of Mary, say the holy doctors, which hastened the coming of God upon the earth; the prayer of Mary made the Holy Spirit, which renewed the earth, descend upon the world. It is the powerful mediation of Mary which sustains the just, raises sinners, and snatches the infidel nations from the wicked empire of Satan.

The lot of Joseph.—What did he do at Nazareth? Like Jesus and Mary, he suffered, labored, and prayed.

It is the lot of the angels and saints in heaven. It is the lot of the elect upon earth; let it be ours too.

Practices.—1. To think, when we recite our daily prayer, *Our Father*, that we are speaking to God, not only for ourselves, but for all men; and that, too, with *one* heart with Jesus Christ, our brother.

2. To unite ourselves to the perpetual sacrifice of Jesus Christ.

3. To say often, with an intention of zeal, which embraces all the necessities of the Church: O Eternal Father! I offer thee the precious blood of Jesus Christ, in satisfaction for my sins, and for the wants of holy Church. (100 days' indulgence, every time.—Pius vii, 1817.)

What good would you not do, if you entered generously into the spirit of the apostleship!

Union with the Perpetual Sacrifice of Jesus Christ.

It is an infinitely consoling fact, and one too little noticed by Christians, that not a single moment of the day or night passes when the spotless Lamb is not sacrificed, on a vast number of altars, for the salvation of the world. What the prophet Malachi foretold is accomplished: "From the rising of the sun, even to the going down, my name is great among the Gentiles, and in every place there is sacrifice, and there is offered to my name a clean oblation." (Malachi, i, 11.) While Europe is enveloped in the darkness of the night, in America, China, and Oceanica, thousands of priests and holy missionaries are offering the holy sacrifice to God.

Christians! you have a very real share in each of these offerings of the divine Victim, and you do not think of it! You owe to God profound homage—to his adorable Majesty, unceasing thanksgivings for his benefits constantly renewed; you owe him reparation for your faults, repeated as often as they have been pardoned: you have an immense and continual need of his graces: and Jesus Christ offers himself every moment to be your sacrifice of adoration, thanksgiving, expiation, and impetration, and you neglect to avail yourself of his offer!

Meantime souls are lost, crimes are multiplied, rumors of wars do not cease, and the Church is threatened: and Jesus Christ invites you to unite yourself with his perpetual sacrifice, in order to ward off these scourges, and you pay no attention to his invitation!

Who does not perceive the fruit which a faithful heart can receive, from uniting its labors and trials, that is, its own daily immolation, with the unceasing and real sacrifice of our Lord Jesus Christ.

Practical Advice on the Way of Making our Evening Prayer.

Sunday Evening.

If there is no benediction of the Blessed Sacrament, it will be well to meditate on the Gospel of the day.

Monday Evening.

We recommend for Monday evening, when there is no office for the dead, that you should reflect on the sense and spirit of any one of your prayers.

This exercise is very profitable and very easy; it consists in taking a vocal prayer: Our Father, Hail, Mary; My God, I acknowledge myself unworthy; one of the commandments of the community, etc., and in weighing, and, as it were, tasting the words, not leaving the first to pass on to the second, until it furnishes us no more thoughts or feelings. You can recall, on this subject, the paraphrase of the *Our Father*.

When the meditation of two or three words is sufficient to fill up the time of our prayer, it is fitting to recite the remainder of the prayer, which you can take up, another time, at the place where you left off. When you have any difficulty with one prayer, you can take another which is more fruitful in reflections.

It is, as it were, indispensable to have the text of these prayers before your eyes to fix your attention, and to follow the most essential points of the subject.

If you succeed well with this exercise, you

can make it more frequently: for instance, on Wednesday morning, you can meditate, from time to time, on the *Athanasian Creed*, the *Universal Prayer;* on Friday, on the *Litany of the Passion;* on confession days, you can paraphrase the beautiful act of contrition in the evening prayers; and on the days of holy communion, on some hymn in honor of the Most Blessed Sacrament.

Tuesday Evening.

DUTIES OF THE SCHOOL.

It is not enough for us to be good religious; we must oblige ourselves, also, to become good teachers. We cannot, in truth, secure our salvation except by laboring for that of the children whom we have to educate. We must, therefore, often meditate on the important duties which we have toward youth, in order to excite ourselves to discharge them well.

Nothing is more profitable than to consider, in our prayer, the sublime nature of our office, its importance, the necessity and the means of fulfilling it well, and the rewards which it can merit for us.

At least, then, once a week, let us meditate on the duties of the school.

Wednesday Evening.

MEDITATION ON ANY CHOSEN SUBJECT.

One of the ends which we propose by leaving a free choice of a subject, and in not making on this day the public reading, is to place you under the necessity of seeking for yourself a subject suited to your personal needs.

As you have often been told, meditation is a remedy for the soul: it is for each one to choose what corresponds best to his spiritual necessities.

The main thing is always to have a definite subject, and to have determined beforehand the book which you will make use of to fix your attention.

It would be very wise and useful to consult the director as to the nature of the subjects which you should generally choose. His experience, the knowledge which he has of your heart, the lights which God gives him for your direction, will enable him to guide you prudently.

Thursday Evening.

VISIT TO THE MOST BLESSED SACRAMENT.

To make this exercise well, you may proceed as follows:—

1. Say *Our Father, Hail, Mary, Glory be to the Father*, six times, so as to gain the indulgences granted to all those who wear the holy scapular of the Immaculate Conception.

2. Adore Jesus Christ, and honor his divine presence in your midst.

3. Thank him for the communions which you have had the happiness of receiving, and particularly for that of the morning.

4. Oblige yourself to make reparation for the outrages which Jesus Christ receives in the sacrament of his love, and make special amends for the injury inflicted on him by religious, who, from negligence, abstain from communion, or make it with tepidity.

5. Unite yourself interiorly with the holy angels, who are constantly prostrate and humbled, at the foot of the altar, in presence of the Immaculate Lamb; unite yourself, also, with all the pious persons who, at this moment, are paying our Lord the same homage as yourself.

6. Look upon yourself as a deputy, in the name of the community, appointed to return thanks to our Lord for the graces which he is pleased to lavish on its members, and particularly for his goodness in giving himself to them so frequently. Ask for the assistance necessary to correspond with these blessings;

and, particularly, beg for yourself and all your brethren a true love for our Lord in the Holy Eucharist; and the grace of always approaching it with holy dispositions, and of deriving therefrom abundant and lasting fruit.

Friday Evening.

THE WAY OF THE CROSS.

Saturday Evening.

REVIEW OF THE WEEK.

The *review of the week* is the natural complement of the annual and monthly retreat.

It is the quickest, surest, and most active remedy to free us from the rust of mere habit, to revive the spirit of faith in us, to renew ourselves in the fulfilment of our duties, and to make known to us where we are, in regard to the reformation of our heart.

"This review," says Fr. de Ravignan, "is a powerful means of sanctification. It makes us enter into ourselves, run rapidly through all the days that are passed, and prove the steps made in the way or out of the way, in order to reanimate ourselves always by submitting to the divine will.

"Experience has proved that many souls have so preserved the strength, light, and peace, which were necessary for the combat of each day, and, sometimes, of each hour."

Manner of Making the Review of the Week.

Invoke, in a special manner, the light of the Holy Ghost.

Put yourself under the protection of the Most Blessed Virgin, of St. Joseph, and of your holy patrons.

Read attentively the resolutions made at your annual or monthly retreat.

Examine whether you have gone backward or forward in comparison with the last week, and search for the cause of your failures, and the means to be employed to amend yourself.

Here is what may be the material of your examen. Lay more stress on what corresponds to your personal needs; insist more or less on it according to the wants of your soul.

Manner of the Examen for the Review of the Week.

Spiritual Exercises.—Have I omitted any by my own fault? Have I made them with application, recollection, and edification?

With what care have I made my meditation? Have I taken practical means to draw much fruit from this exercise?

How have I heard holy Mass? What profit have I derived from it? With what intention have I assisted at it?

Have I been to confession this week? Have I done this from custom, without preparation, without a desire of amendment, and without any care to excite myself to contrition for my faults?

Have I omitted communion? Have I prepared myself with care, and, especially, with some sacrifice made each time for this end? Have I divided the time, according to the example of the saints, between the preparation and thanksgiving?

What use have I made of spiritual communion?

Have I nothing to reproach myself with, regarding my morning or evening prayers, or the beads? Have I said the little prayers with piety and devotion?

Has my spiritual reading been really spiritual reading? Has the study of the catechism been well made?

Have I made my examens well, especially the particular examen? Have I been faithful in marking down the result? Has not the examen of foresight been neglected?

What use have I made of ejaculatory prayers—of the holy exercise of the presence of God?

Care of perfection.—What efforts have I made to advance in perfection, to correct my bad inclinations, especially my predominant passion; to reform my character, and to practise the essential virtues, as humility, chastity, poverty, obedience, mortification?

Does there not exist in me an inclination to venial sin, on any point? Have I not allowed myself many faults, under the pretext that they were trifling?

Am I recollected, and modest with my eyes in going through the streets, in church, etc.?

How have I made the examination of conscience?

Have I well understood the sad consequences of such and such steps, of such and such inclinations? Have I combated them?

Employment.—How have I acquitted myself of my office? Have I done this negligently or with fervor—with the spirit of faith or with natural views?

What misery, if, acting by routine and with human views, I lose the merit of my trials and labors!

How have I given the catechism and reflection?

Have I watched well over my pupils?
Have I always given them edification? Have
they not lost time through my fault?

Have the prayers been well recited in
school?

Community-life.—How have I behaved
with reference to the superior? Have I regarded God in his person? Have I a true
charity for all my brothers? Have I not
some familiarity, coldness, or vehemence, to
reproach myself with? Do I see in all my
brethren the members of Jesus Christ? Have
I edified everybody by the practice of modesty, silence, and the faithful observance of
the rule?

How have I behaved during recreation?

Have I sanctified my meals by some mortifications?

Have I employed well the time devoted
to study and the preparation of my lessons?
May I not have been a cause of distraction
and trouble to others?

What a misery, if I have to give an account,
not only of my own faults, but also of those
of my brothers!

After this examination, humbly beg pardon of God for all the faults and negligences
which you have remarked in yourself. Far
from being discouraged, make salutary and

very definite resolutions for the next week. Do not say, I will be more fervent; but say: I will apply myself particularly to correct such a fault, to practise such a virtue under such circumstances, and to make this exercise in that manner, etc. Foresee, also, the means which you have to employ to attain this object. See if you should not change the subject of your particular examen: this exercise, well done, will be the principal means of rooting out your faults, and causing you to advance in perfection.

Note down, if needful, the principal faults which you have noticed, and the resolutions which you have made.

Mark down, also, the general result of the week, on the page destined for that purpose.

Offer to our Lord your communion of the following day, in reparation for the faults of the week, and to obtain the grace of being faithful to the resolutions which you have just made.

Finish this exercise, by invoking the aid of your holy patrons, of your guardian angel, and, especially, of the most blessed Virgin; and beg, by their intercession, the grace of a generous renewal for yourself and your brethren

METHOD OF HEARING MASS;

OR, PIOUS PRACTICES

*By means of which you may derive great benefit from assisting at the Holy Sacrifice.**

BEFORE MASS.

ON your way to the church, consider that you are going to Calvary, there to witness the most sublime and affecting spectacle that can be imagined, that of a God-made man, who immolates himself on a cross, suspended between heaven and earth, in order to reconcile earth with heaven, and man with God. Consider with lively faith that the sacrifice of the Mass is the renewal of that of the cross, or, rather, that it *is*, according to the Council of Trent, the same sacrifice, with this sole difference, that, on the altar, it is accomplished without the shedding of blood, and that consequently it produces the same effects, since the Victim and He who sacrifices are the same, Jesus Christ, who, by the ministry of His priests, offers Himself to God His Father.

These considerations should inspire you, while on your way to the church, with sentiments of reverence, confidence, and devotion.

Having entered the church, and chosen a place where you may be free from distractions, resolve to avoid those faults which you are liable to commit when assisting at Mass, and beg of God the grace to be faithful to your resolutions. You will then express your desire to attain the ends for which the Holy Sacrifice is offered, namely, to render to God the honor due to Him in acknowledgment of His supreme dominion over all

---

* Excerpt from NEW PRACTICAL MEDITATIONS FOR EVERY DAY IN THE YEAR, by Rev. Bruno Vercruysse, S.J. 2 vols., 12mo, cloth, beveled, red edges. $5. Benziger Bros., New-York, Cincinnati, and St. Louis.

creatures; to obtain from His infinite goodness mercy and forgiveness of your sins; to thank Him for the innumerable benefits received from Him, and to implore a continuance of His favors.

DURING MASS.

There are many ways by which you may secure to yourself the fruits of the Holy Sacrifice. Much latitude is left, on this point, to the devotion of the faithful. Some use the prayers for Mass to be found in any of the Prayer-Books, while others prefer to recite the Rosary or the Litanies, with pious exercises suited for every day in the week, or else the Office of the Dead, the Little Office of the Blessed Virgin, or that of the Sacred Heart. Choose those prayers which seem best to you, taking care, however, that these vocal exercises do not so occupy you as to exclude the consideration of the three principal parts of the Mass: the *Offertory*, *Consecration*, and *Communion*. Adopt for these precious moments some fixed practices of devotion, which may assist you to participate largely in the graces attached to them. A few may be here suggested:

1st. At the OFFERTORY. Whilst the priest elevates the Host on the paten, pronouncing the words, *Suscipe, Sancte Pater, hanc immaculatam Hostiam*, "Accept, Holy Father, this unspotted Host," unite your offering to his; place yourself in spirit on the altar of sacrifice, and say from your heart, Deign, Heavenly Father, to receive the offering which I humbly make to Thee of my body and soul, with all their senses and faculties. They are the gifts of Thy bounty. To Thee do I surrender them, and I declare before the holy angels who now surround this altar, that I desire to use them only in conformity with Thy holy will made manifest in Thy commandments. My most fervent wish is to belong wholly to Thee, and to devote myself in all things to the advancement of the glory of Thy Holy Name, to the salvation of others, and to my own sanctification.

Sustain me by Thy grace, I entreat Thee, O Father of Mercy! that I may persevere to my last breath in these dispositions. Having thus prayed and offered yourself to God, make a brief examination, considering how far your conduct has hitherto corresponded with the profession you have just made, in order that you may henceforth prove more faithful.

2d. The CONSECRATION or ELEVATION. At this solemn moment, when the priest elevates before the congregation the Divine Victim concealed under the appearance of the consecrated Host, contemplate with lively faith your beloved Saviour, as He was beheld by those who had nailed Him to the cross, covered with blood and wounded for your sins, and in the midst of His agonizing pain, forgetting Himself to plead your cause with His Father, and to implore pardon for you in that cry which He uttered from His heart, *Pater, dimitte illis*, " Father, forgive them."

This contemplation should inspire you with lively sentiments of admiration, love, and gratitude, with horror of sin, contrition, and boundless devotion.

Having expressed these sentiments, unite with Jesus in the prayer which He offered to His heavenly Father on behalf of all mankind, contemplate in succession the five wounds which are, as St. Bonaventure says: "so many places of refuge, so many voices raised in supplication, to intercede for us," and at each one ask some particular grace or favor.

At the wound of the right hand: Pray for the Sovereign Pontiff, and for those bishops, priests, and missionaries who labor under his direction for the salvation of souls, that their zealous exertions may be crowned with the fullest success. At the wound of the left hand: Pray for the conversion of heathens, Jews, heretics, and schismatics, and for the return to God of all bad Christians who are in league with hell against Jesus Christ and His Holy Church. At the wound of the right foot: Pray for the members of your family, beginning with those most closely connected by affinity; for your benefactors and friends; and likewise, as Christ ordains, for your enemies. At the wound of the left foot: Pray for the souls in Purgatory, particularly those who have most claims on your charity. At the wound of the heart of Jesus: Pray for yourself; place in that heart, burning with love, all your cares, troubles, fears, hopes, and desires.

By adopting the habit of thus offering your petitions in a certain order, corresponding with the five wounds of Our Divine Lord, you will always be able, in a few moments, and without effort, to offer an universal prayer, pleasing to God, and most beneficial to your neighbor and yourself.

3d. The COMMUNION. On those days when you have not the happiness of approaching the holy table, you should not neglect to make a *spiritual communion*, which, according to Saint Teresa, "is sometimes as advantageous as actual communion." This consists in forming in your heart with great devotion, three acts, namely, an act of contrition, as nearly perfect as possible; an act of charity or love of God; and an act of ardent desire to approach the Holy Communion and derive from it the abundant graces which it confers on those who prepare to receive it worthily.

AFTER MASS.

Examine briefly:

If you have followed exactly the preceding counsels.

How you have employed the intervals of time which separate the principal parts of the Holy Sacrifice.

If you have been careful as to your exterior deportment, and vigilant in avoiding distractions.

If all has been well done, return thanks to God: if otherwise, ask pardon for your negligence. Before leaving the holy place, beg of Jesus to bless all your occupations during the coming day, as well as the good resolutions that you have made during morning prayer or meditation.

Sent free by mail on receipt of price.

NEW PRACTICAL MEDITATIONS

FOR EVERY DAY IN THE YEAR,
ON THE LIFE OF OUR LORD JESUS CHRIST.

Chiefly intended for the Use of Religious Communities.

By the Rev. Father BRUNO VERCRUYSSE, S.J.

The only complete English translation. Published with the approbation and under the direction of the author.

Enriched by several Novenas and Octaves; Meditations for the First Friday of every month and for the Days of Communion; Exercises preparatory to the Renewal of Vows, and for a Retreat of Eight Days; a New Method of Hearing Mass, and Practical Remarks on the Different Parts of Meditations; a Plan of Jerusalem, with a Map of Palestine, showing the different Localities mentioned throughout the Work, and an Alphabetical Table of Contents and of Meditations on the Gospels of the Sundays.

2 vols., 1244 pp. Extra cloth, bevelled boards, red edges, $5.

The merit of this work is established by the many editions through which it has passed—no less than 19,000 copies having been printed in different languages, within six years—as also, by the approbations it has received from the ecclesiastical authorities and from the SUPERIOR-GENERAL OF THE SOCIETY OF JESUS.

The Meditations are short but thoroughly practical, and will be found invaluable to the Reverend Clergy, as they furnish ample material for homilies on the Gospels and for sermons on the feasts of the year, and the principal points of morals. The feasts of the several founders of religious orders are in the second volume arranged according to their dates.

A PRAYER BEFORE MEDITATION and some admirable REMARKS ON THE CONSIDERATIONS are printed separately, on a loose sheet of heavy paper, and accompany each volume, serving the purpose of a book-mark.

In connection with the above, we have issued an excellent

METHOD OF HEARING MASS,

of a form suitable for inserting in prayer books. It is extensively circulated in Europe, in the academies and colleges. Price, 50 cents per 100.

BENZIGER BROTHERS, New York, Cincinnati, and St. Louis.

FOR THE
CHILDREN OF CATHOLIC SCHOOLS.

CONTAINING A

MASS IN VERSICLES AND RESPONSES;

To be read aloud, with a view to

FIXING the ATTENTION of the CHILDREN.

48mo, 192 pp.   Imitation Cloth, full Gilt Sides and Back.

Fully Illustrated.   20 cents.

Every attentive parent or teacher has remarked how few of the many children who attend at the Holy Sacrifice really know how "to hear Mass." To do this with the proper dispositions they must be taught the meaning of the different parts of the Mass, be impressed with its solemnity, and learn how to use their prayer-books so as to follow the priest at the Altar. Their levity must be held in check, and some means adopted to **fix their attention on the Adorable Sacrifice which is being offered.** To effect this latter, a MASS IN VERSICLES AND RESPONSES, to be read aloud, and which *calls for constant attention* has been adopted. The plan has long been in use in Europe, where it has proved most efficient; but although the want of such a book has been greatly felt and earnestly demanded, until now it has never been presented in English. This Mass, which is adapted to young minds, has been taken, as far as practicable, from the Roman Missal, and is calculated to fulfill its end in an agreeable and edifying manner.

Morning and Evening Prayers and other devotions in general use have been added, and many beautiful initial letters and other illustrations.

A liberal discount made for introduction.

BENZIGER BROTHERS, New York, Cincinnati, and St. Louis.

Sent free by mail, on receipt of price

THE IMITATION
OF THE
Sacred Heart of Jesus.

By Rev. F. ARNOUDT, S.J.

TRANSLATED FROM THE LATIN OF REV. J. M. FASTRE.

12mo, 798 pages, extra cloth, $2.50.

———o———

This delightful book contains ample matter for daily meditation throughout the year. The reader can start from the beginning and continue to the end of the work, or he may break this order and confine himself to such portions as are specially adapted to his feelings at the time. Things are not proposed here in general and in common, as is usually done in books of meditation, but everything is laid down specially and in particular, both in regard to the evil to be avoided, and the good to be practiced. The book greatly resembles the "Imitation of Christ," to which it is a fitting companion, but it is more regular in plan, more complete, actual, definite. The style of the work is everywhere suited to the subject, and the diction is pure.

———o———

The Hidden Treasure;
OR, THE VALUE AND EXCELLENCE OF
THE HOLY MASS.
WITH A
Practical and Devout Method of Hearing it with Profit.

By The Blessed Leonard of Port-Maurice.

18mo, 188 pages, cloth, 50 cents.

BENZIGER BROTHERS, New York, Cincinnati, and St. Louis.

THE LIFE OF
Our Lord and Saviour Jesus Christ and of His Blessed Mother.

Translated and Adapted from the original of Rev. L. C. BUSINGER, by

REV. RICHARD BRENNAN, LL.D.,
Author of "A Popular Life of Pope Pius IX."

Large 4to. To be completed in 38 parts, at

25 cents

each. Illustrated with nearly 600 engravings, 6 beautiful Chromo-Lithographs, 31 full-page, fine Plates, a handsome Illuminated Title-page, a Presentation Plate and a Family Record, printed in colors. In addition, each subscriber is presented free with a superb steel engraving ($20\frac{1}{2} \times 27\frac{1}{2}$ inches) of "THE RESURRECTION OF OUR LORD."

The Work is approved by

HIS EMINENCE, THE CARDINAL, ARCHBISHOP OF NEW YORK,

The Most Reverend Archbishops of
CINCINNATI,—MILWAUKEE,—PHILADELPHIA,—PORTLAND, OREGON,—QUEBEC,—ST. BONIFACE, MANITOBA,—TORONTO;

The Right Reverend Bishops of
ALBANY,—ARIZONA,—BROOKLYN,—CHARLOTTETOWN, P. E. I.,—COVINGTON,—ERIE,—FORT WAYNE,—GERMANICOPOLIS, —GRASS VALLEY,—GREEN BAY,—HARBOR GRACE, N. F.,— JAMAICA, W. I.,—LA CROSSE,—LITTLE ROCK,—LONDON, ONT.,—MARQUETTE,—OTTAWA, P. Q.,—PROVIDENCE,— SAVANNAH,—SHERBROOKE, P. Q.,—ST. ALBERT, HUDSON'S BAY TER.,—ST. CLOUD,—ST. HYACINTHE, P. Q.,—WHEELING.

SOLD ONLY BY SUBSCRIPTION.

BENZIGER BROTHERS, New York, Cincinnati, and St. Louis.

Pictorial Lives of the Saints.

WITH REFLECTIONS, FOR EVERY DAY IN THE YEAR,
AND A PREFACE BY

REV. EDWARD McGLYNN, D.D.,
Pastor of St. Stephen's Church, New York.

Illustrated with nearly **400 Engravings**, depicting striking passages in the lives of these Servants of God. 1 vol., 8vo.

Elegantly bound in extra cloth, full gilt side.......... $3 50
" " " " " " and edges, 4 00
" " " in French morocco, " " 5 50

Approved by

HIS EMINENCE, THE CARDINAL, ARCHBISHOP OF NEW YORK,

The Most Reverend Archbishops of
MILWAUKEE,—PHILADELPHIA,—PORTLAND, OREGON.

And the Right Reverend Bishops of
ARIZONA,—BUFFALO,—COLUMBUS,—CHICAGO,—CLEVELAND,—ERIE,—FORT WAYNE,—GALVESTON,—GERMANICOPOLIS,—GRASS VALLEY,—GREEN BAY,—LEAVENWORTH,—LOUISVILLE,—NESQUALY,—OGDENSBURGH,—PEORIA,—PROVIDENCE,—SAVANNAH,—SCRANTON,—ST. CLOUD,—ST. PAUL,—WHEELING.

SOLD ONLY BY SUBSCRIPTION.

———

A Popular Life of

POPE PIUS THE NINTH.

Drawn from the most reliable authorities by
REV. RICHARD BRENNAN, A.M.

Approved by His Eminence
CARDINAL McCLOSKEY AND ELEVEN BISHOPS.

1 vol., small 8vo.

Elegantly bound in cloth, gilt extra................. $1 50
" " " " extra gilt edges............ 2 00

BENZIGER BROTHERS, New York, Cincinnati, and St. Louis.

www.ingramcontent.com/pod-product-compliance
Lightning Source LLC
Chambersburg PA
CBHW031327230426
43670CB00006B/264